AF412202

Future

Anterior

Future Anterior
Volume XIII, Number 1
Summer 2016

Preservation in a World of Diplomacy

The ongoing destruction of cultural heritage by Islamic State (IS) in Syria and Iraq brings to the fore a glaring paradox. On the one hand, preventing the deliberate destruction of culture now appears to hold little moral ambiguity, with such acts now regularly condemned by various governments and agencies around the world as both "war crimes" and a "crimes against humanity." And yet, the failure to prevent IS's campaign of destruction is a stark reminder of the vulnerabilities of culture in times of conflict, and the inability of the so-called international community to act upon the imperative to preserve. Indeed, today it appears as though the threat to cultural heritage is increasing in magnitude in accordance with the changing nature of international conflict and terrorism.

Looking across Western media, academia, and the various agencies committed to preventing further destruction, the response to IS has revolved around select themes, namely the legal instruments for preventing the illicit trafficking of objects, the challenges of protecting archaeological sites and museum collections, or the benefits of documentation and digital capture. While fully recognizing the critical importance of such efforts, I would, however, suggest that the challenge posed by IS extends beyond questions of actual preservation and international law, to include a serious diplomatic conundrum, one that has not received the critical and sustained attention it deserves.

We have come a long way since World War II, and yet the characteristics of today's international relations and diplomatic arena mean significant challenges remain in putting together effective solutions to a phenomenon like IS. UNESCO has led the charge in raising awareness of the plight of the region's cultural heritage, and the issue has received sporadic attention from a number of governments around the world. In September 2014, for example, U.S. Secretary of State John Kerry announced that the Department of State would dedicate resources for preservation and documentation of heritage in the region. In May 2015, ninety-one states supported the UN General Assembly Resolution "Saving the Cultural Heritage of Iraq" (69/281). With the protection of culture now widely acknowledged as a human rights issue, it would appear it is the responsibility of all to act. This idealism, however, belies the far more complex task of bringing together "coalitions of

Future Anterior
Volume XIII, Number 1
Summer 2016

the willing." For Syria and Iraq's regional neighbors, material culture inherited from the past is deeply entangled in the broader politics of the region today and speaks to the hostilities between Sunni and Shiite groups and the religious roots at the heart of tensions between countries such as Saudi Arabia and Iran. The possibility for enacting effective heritage protection interventions in Syria has been further complicated by the domestic political situation, whereby IS has provided a geopolitically expedient foil for Bashar al-Assad. In this regard, both Syria and Iraq also raise the highly challenging question of how to intervene in the protection of culture when states collapse and domestic governmental priorities shift in other directions.

Although IS's version of Wahhabi extremism, which attempts to erase the cultural pasts of others, bears the hallmarks of nation-building, their declared aim to establish a caliphate is an explicit attempt to stand outside the current international system of nation-states. The situation presents major challenges for both states and intergovernmental agencies searching for diplomatic solutions to the heritage issue. With so much of the focus on the destruction of high-profile sites such as Palmyra and Nimrud, we also need to ask why far less concern has been expressed in the Western media over the destruction of Syria's mosques, churches, and other shrines, or to the extensive damage to the historic cities of Yemen caused by Saudi Arabian air attacks. Equally, with much of the burden seeming to rest on the shoulders of UNESCO, what should we expect from the Islamic Educational, Scientific and Cultural Organization (ISESCO) in steering more effective political, legal, and "on the ground" policies? The pursuit of such lines of enquiry adds clarity to a situation wherein the protection of culture and heritage appears to be a largely uncontentious enterprise with a clear moral imperative but nevertheless remains bound up in complex political, geopolitical, and diplomatic relations—factors that greatly complicate the process of both conceiving and implementing meaningful and efficacious responses.

The current situation in the Middle East bears heavily upon the themes raised in this special issue. Although the various essays gathered here do not directly address the conflict in Syria and Iraq, they help open new questions and lines of enquiry around international heritage governance and the politics of its preservation. Conflicts pose important questions about cooperation: How do you more effectively assemble partners and coalitions? In what ways does a shared cultural heritage create both political alignments and enmities? How, precisely, does preservation come to be enacted via a network of nation-states, nongovernmental agencies, and intergovernmental organizations today? This special issue on preservation and diplomacy explores such themes. It does so not by addressing the pragmatics of diplomatic interventions but by teasing out connections and themes that arise when you consider preservation through a lens of diplomacy.

It is important to note here, then, that the concept of diplomacy is used in a broad sense to open up the analysis of preservation at the international level in ways that incorporate ideas about international relations and governance. The aim is to reveal how heritage preservation takes on particular structures and forms as it intersects with the logics and mechanisms that constitute the political relations of international discourse. In that regard, the articles that follow from part of a larger concern for expanding our accounts of international preservation and its history, toward themes that have hitherto not received the critical attention they deserve. To that end, elsewhere I have explored heritage diplomacy as an approach that can more carefully read how the internationalization of preservation — as both an ethos and an institutional landscape — has occurred in the modern era and what role it has played in the story of globalization. Heritage diplomacy seeks to add nuance to our understanding of the ways the relations among governments, civil society organizations, and intergovernmental agencies shape the arena of preservation at the international level. Keeping the nation-state as a key focus, it also points to the importance and analytical insights that can arise by inserting the hyphen into the inter-national.

This special issue of *Future Anterior* develops such themes further by examining the links between preservation and diplomacy across a number of different geographic and historic contexts, including North Africa, Asia, Europe, the Middle East, and North America. To highlight the importance of reading preservation and diplomacy in analytically broad terms, this issue also moves between a series of scales and registers, and features discussions about World Heritage meetings, borders, foreign policies, or the issues that arise when preserving politically charged archaeological sites or overseas buildings.

Mindful that no single special issue can lay claim to comprehensive coverage, the idea of assembling the particular articles that follow rests upon the premise that important analytical work still needs to be done to better understand the various factors and forces that determine where and when preservation occurs and what forms it takes. Somewhat strangely, material culture rarely features in studies undertaken by scholars working in the fields of international relations and political science. This neglect is also somewhat surprising given recent debates concerning the need to conceive diplomacy in more expansive ways. The 2013 *Oxford Handbook of*

Modern Diplomacy, for example, featured chapters on media, food, refugee, health, sport, and climate diplomacies, an approach that explicitly recognized how diplomatic culture and practice can permeate the conduct of various international sectors today. A key implication here, then, is the need to ask more reaching questions about who actually conducts diplomatic activities and takes on ambassadorial roles, and what other contexts and arenas we might consider as exhibiting the qualities of international diplomacy. If we bring cultural heritage and preservation into this picture, fascinating questions arise. It has been suggested that cultural diplomacy is most effective when conducted by nonstate actors. In the U.S. preservation sector, then, we might ask the degree to which organizations such as the Getty Conservation Institute, World Monuments Fund, or Smithsonian Institute are engaged in international diplomatic practice. I would suggest they, along with the Washington-based Cultural Ambassadors Fund for Cultural Preservation and Antiquities Coalition, constitute a landscape of heritage diplomacy that supports and advances U.S. bilateral relations around the world today. As this issue demonstrates, however, the United States is far from alone in this regard, such that numerous countries now have an array of state and nonstate agencies involved in preservation aid, oriented around a variety of bi- and multilateral collaborations. It is a line of enquiry that suggests we also need to more closely consider how preservation, and the provision of heritage aid, constitutes forms of hard or soft power. Equally, and perhaps most urgently, we can also more precisely enquire into the role heritage preservation plays—or might play—in developing more productive inter-national and cross-cultural relations. Ongoing conflict in the Middle East and the specter of international terrorism suggest the need to ask far more ambitious and challenging questions about culture and cultural heritage and their capacity for creating conflict and distrust, as well as dialogue, respect, and humility. I would suggest that comprehending where both possibilities and traps might lie requires a more nuanced and robust understanding of how the preservation sector, its technologies, institutions, funding structures, and projects, are both entangled in and absent from those larger political, diplomatic relations that make up the structures and channels of international security and global governance today.

To bring these various threads together, then, the aim of connecting preservation with diplomacy is twofold. First, it can help us better understand the role preservation and cultural heritage have played, and continue to play, in international affairs and relations. Second, it can bring to light the key ways those relations and wider structures of international governance have shaped the preservation sector itself. Most of the essays here stem from discussions and conference panels I convened in 2014 and 2015. Early drafts by Akagawa, Clarke, James, Swenson, and Yapp formed part of a panel on "Heritage Diplomacy" at the Association of Critical Heritage Studies conference in Canberra, Australia. The papers by Carruthers and Winter were first presented during a panel on "Heritage Diplomacy and Networks of Conservation Knowledge" at an international conference on Knowledge Transfer and Cultural Exchanges in Lisbon, Portugal. Given the theme of the issue, we were also excited that Jane Loeffler and Diane Siebrandt accepted invitations to contribute an article and book review, respectively, on different, yet intricately connected, aspects of U.S. preservation diplomacy.

In This Issue

Future Anterior
Volume XIII, Number 1
Summer 2016

War II. Taking the example of Vietnam as one of the recipients of Japan's cultural aid, it demonstrates how international support for heritage projects has played a central role in the ideological and economic processes of nation building and soft power.

Artist Intervention: *The Controlled Ruin:* Preserving Collective Memories through Building Transformation
Mo Michelsen Stochholm Krag
Since the 1950s, social migration from rural Denmark toward its urban areas has resulted in abandoned villages. This project outlines the transformation of an abandoned building pro-totyped at full scale in a rural village setting. This particular transformation was implemented as an attempt to catalyze an exchange of memories of the building and the place as an alternative to demolition.

1. *Monument to the Third International* by Vladimir Tatlin. Model in the courtyard of the Royal Academy London. Photograph by author.

Astrid Swenson

The First Heritage International(s)
Conceptualizing Global Networks before UNESCO

Future Anterior
Volume XIII, Number 1
Summer 2016

Attitudes toward heritage have long been a subject of national rather than international history. Recent years, however, have seen a remarkable growth of scholarship with a global perspective.[1] In this literature, UNESCO's role has been particularly central through a proliferation of institutional histories and discursive critiques, and as part of broader historicization of international institutions as transnational sites.[2] Understanding the effect of UNESCO on the ground, however, remains, according to Jean-François Sirinelli, chair of the independent International Scientific Committee for the history of UNESCO, "une histoire à suivre."[3] There also is a need to widen the focus to understand the governance of heritage as an aspect of globalization in the era since World War II more broadly. As Tim Winter pointed out,

> we have yet to detail the story of the ongoing dance that has taken place between nationalisms and the ethos of cosmopolitan internationalism in shaping the global expansion of institutionalized conservation. As a consequence, the analytical frames capable of making sense of the systemic problems that now face the flagship of heritage conservation, the World Heritage movement, still need to be constructed.[4]

I propose to take this historicization one step further and place the postwar developments in their longer trajectory. In this article I will suggest ways of conceptualizing heritage internationalism before UNESCO. Heritage internationalism remains often seen as a relatively recent phenomenon, linked to the wish to overcome nationalist approaches to culture after the Second World War and "to build peace in the minds of men".[5] But its roots go much deeper. A number of international movements formed through diplomatic and civil efforts beginning in the late eighteenth century. Some pursued the idea of world heritage; others were more focused on strengthening national heritage through likeminded international alliances. Yet all reveal that international and national agendas have been in constant tension for more than two centuries.[6]

Many "critical heritage scholars" have chastised modern heritage internationalism, and UNESCO in particular, for imposing a Western heritage concept on the rest of the world, thereby perpetuating the legacies of colonial dispossession.[7] Although

1

the emergence of heritage concepts and heritage institutions were deeply linked to the history of imperialism, they were made not only by Western elites but through the interactions of a range of actors from a variety of social and ethnic backgrounds.[8] For a more rounded picture it is necessary to reflect not only on acts of dominance but also on subversive as well as collaborative approaches. By adopting a long chronological perspective and by paying attention to the multiplicity of international networks and international interactions that coexisted, the article aims to help understanding the role heritage played in the transformation of the modern world and vice versa.[9] By doing so, it also hopes to advance comprehension of contemporary developments: First, by showing that the international making of heritage has deeper, more complex, and less linear histories than generally thought, it invites to reflect on how the legacies of these histories still shape current attitudes. Second, by looking at a period in which no single institution represented heritage interests internationally like UNESCO does today, the article also proposes that a similar multiactor perspective could be fruitful for the analysis of the present. Finally, it suggests that it is necessary to pay more attention to the strength of individual agency and not to assume that all forms of heritage internationalism derive automatically from a hegemonic or even coherent "authorized" discourse.[10] Rather, it proposes to understand how the international sphere, despite unequal power relations, functioned as both a "site" and a "resource" for different actors.[11]

Looking at a period that did not possess a formal international institution, or even the word *heritage* in its current broad meaning, poses obvious methodological challenges with regard to how widely one casts the net. For the sake of offering a long-term perspective, I am operating here with a broad twenty-first-century definition of heritage in cultural and natural, tangible and intangible terms to capture a historic phenomenon often referred to by contemporaries in different words. This does not mean to negate important conceptual differences, but to highlight how concerns about different forms of what we would now call heritage developed and interacted with each other at particular moments in time.[12]

Despite the growth of transnational histories of preservation over the past years, the mapping of transnational, let alone global, networks of preservation is still very much a work in progress. Few, if any, of the studies that engage with connections beyond the nation are truly global in the sense of offering comprehensive coverage. Rather, they approach global connections through particular localities. Given the gaps in research, it is still too early for a synthesis. There are, however, now enough studies on different periods and geographical contexts to think about how broader patterns might be conceptualized. In addition to the research on UNESCO's role, and earlier works on conservationist thought and the codification of international law,[13] a range of historical studies has looked at the cross-cultural construction of different aspects of what is now called "heritage."[14] Focusing largely on the nineteenth and early twentieth centuries, these studies show the strength of exchanges across different national and imperial borders from Peru to Japan, as well as the emergence of particular international structures set up to facilitate exchanges. Methodological frameworks differ as a result of disciplinary and linguistic traditions and vary between "comparative," "entangled," "transnational," "transcultural," "imperial," or "global history" approaches. It is not my purpose here to advocate for one over the another. Often methodologies are complementary rather than exclusive.[15] None has a single definition and each can be understood as the broader of churches.[16] All can be fruitfully applied to understand processes rather than spaces. The appropriate method does to some degree depend on particular geographical and temporal context,[17] yet the framework one chooses might determine what kind of connections one sees as dominant in a particular period.

In the face of often overwhelmingly national and nationalist uses of heritage, the primary aim of many studies employing a transnational or cognate methodology has been to establish that connections beyond current national borders existed at all. For many contexts empirical research is, at best, only at the beginning, and it remains important to refute essentializing definitions of heritage by showing how concepts have been changed across cultures through processes of transfer, translation, and transculturation. Yet, it is also time to go beyond the statement that heritage is a concept made in transit. Future analyses will need to compare what happens in cross-cultural processes (do the same or different mechanisms appear and why?) and to think about the relation between the different networks uncovered to reflect whether the contacts that shaped heritage are indeed different, only loosely touching networks or are part of something much more interconnected.

The Heritage Internationals
I titled this article "The First Heritage International(s)" with the plural in brackets to indicate both the existence of a relatively coordinated, coherent, and self-aware movement before the creation of twentieth-century international organizations,[18] as well as the plurality of successive and parallel initiatives. Both "heritage international" and "heritage internationalism," like "heritage diplomacy" are of course contemporary terms. Similar to "heritage diplomacy," "heritage international"

and "heritage internationalism" can help make sense of the "international flow and circulation of ideas, people, funding, and policies in the space of heritage."[19] Often congruent, the different terms can, however, also assist in directing the gaze toward different aspects. While " heritage diplomacy" helps emphasize the process, "heritage international" draws attention to the structures. Moreover, while internationalism shaped *"heritage in diplomacy"* and *"heritage as diplomacy,"* and vice versa,[20] not all international heritage networks had a diplomatic or internationalist function. In contrast to the "Socialist Internationals" from which the term "Heritage Internationals" borrows, the various movements that were concerned with the preservation of the cultural and natural environment, as well as with forms of heritage that we would now call intangible, never labeled themselves as "Internationals." They generally also had much looser forms of formation, affiliation, and dissolution. No monument remembers them like Tatlin's *Monument to the Third International* (Figure 1). By choosing the term, I do not want to suggest that the "Heritage Internationals" were like the "Socialist Internationals";[21] I propose it rather as a metaphor to structure the profusion of international, transnational, and transcultural activities and networks concerned with heritage and to problematize relations. Moreover, like scholars who speak of "religious internationals" to capture the formation of global religious movements during the nineteenth and early twentieth century,[22] I find the term useful to draw attention to the fact that the internationalization of heritage preservation was part of a broader move toward internationalization. While the looseness of networks might not always make the label of "International" with a capital *I* seem fitting, borrowing the idea of successive internationals from the socialists also helps to think about reasons for disruption and continuity in relation to the history of "internationalism in the age of nationalism" more broadly.[23]

Questions about continuity inevitably raise questions about origins. Very different starting points could be chosen. A history of the international and diplomatic uses of heritage could begin in the ancient world (a multitude of incidences from the restoration of Cyrus tomb by Alexander the Great, to Cicero's *In Verrem,* to the various post-antique *translatii imperii* come to mind).[24] Or it could start with the transformation of the international order and the emergence of the diplomatic system in the Early Modern Period.[25] Or with the fundamental changes brought by European expansion since the fifteenth century. But if we are interested in a more self-conscious heritage internationalism, it is best to begin with the late eighteenth century, as it was only in this period that a strong sense of internationalism and of heritage protection first

came together.[26] To frame the debate about the nature of the
heritage internationals, I will therefore begin with movements
that mobilized internationalism to save heritage, or heritage to
champion internationalism, and that had universal aspiration
if not membership. I then will relate these to other forms of
international heritage networks. In the broadest sense, self-
conscious heritage internationalism can be divided into two
periods: a first, between the French Revolution and the First
World War, which was characterized by informal internationalism, and a second, shaped by formal international organization within the frameworks of the League of Nations and the
United Nations.[27] However, it also makes sense to divide the
periodization further, as there were distinct regimes of heritage internationalism reflecting broader shifts in international
relations. I would suggest five main "Internationals" and two
intermediary ones.

Triggered by the spoliation of art works and scientific
objects by the French Revolutionary and Napoleonic Armies,
a "First Heritage International" emerged as a pan-European
effort to return the objects. While not questioning the growing
pillage of works of art and science from outside Europe, this
first heritage international was shaped by the Enlightenment
belief in a common heritage of mankind. As Quatremère de
Quincy put it in his *Letters to Miranda*: "You know that the arts
and sciences have long constituted a republic in Europe. All
political and philosophical efforts must be employed to maintain, strengthen, and augment this community."[28] Ultimately,
the plea for the return of art works was successful, but what
had started as a defense of cosmopolitan values by artists and
writers ended with a diplomatic solution through the Congress
of Vienna in 1815 and the triumph of national understandings
of heritage.[29]

The "Second International" has no single, clear starting
point. In contrast to the First, and the Third and Fourth, it was
not crisis driven. In many ways it started as soon as peace was
established in 1815: learned exchanges were formalized again,
and diplomatic services were used to exchange idea to set up
national heritage-preservation systems across Europe, often
drawing on contacts created during the restitution debate. But
the Second Heritage International's true growth was linked to
the idea of free trade internationalism and the world's fairs and
international congresses, which this idea engendered. Between
the 1870s and 1914, exchanges on heritage were particularly
intense, facilitated by numerous international exhibitions on
preservation, a plethora of international congresses on tangible and intangible forms of heritage, a range of transnational
campaigns to save monuments and natural sites across the
globe, and a drive to codify the protection of works of art,

2. Chen Jitong (1851–1907), Chinese delegate at the 1889 First International Congress for the Protection of Monuments and Works of Art. Photograph by Nadar. Wikimedia CC0 1.0.

history, and science during war. Though dominated by European countries, the Second International's range was broader than the First's and the Third's. Congress representatives, for instance, included Japanese, Chinese, Mexican, and Brazilian delegates (Figure 2).[30]

The First World War, and the willful destruction of Belgian and French artistic treasures by the German army, ended the patterns of this long period of exchange (Figure 3).[31] At the same time, the First World War, like the major nineteenth-century wars before it, reinforced the belief in the necessity of international protection. This manifested on both sides of the conflict. While the German army created its *Kunstschutz* program to disprove allegations of barbarism,[32] civilians from the entente countries solicited the help of (then still) neutral America to formulate protest petitions and met in Geneva to create a "Red Cross for monuments" (Figure 4).[33]

We might call these later initiatives (which replaced Germany with the United States as a major player in the international preservation movement) the "2 1/2 Heritage International" (mixing and matching labels from the social-

3. The Destruction of Reims Cathedral in 1914. *Collier's New Photographic History of the World's War* (New York: Collier's, 1919), 86. Wikimedia Commons. Public domain.

ist Congress at Zimmerwald that stuck to its pacifist aims and refused to accept the dissolution of the Second Socialist International after the European socialist parties had voted in favor of war credits in 1914, and the 2 1/2 international founded as an alternative to Lenin's Third).[34] After the end of World War I, however, a truly new phase of the "Third International" started with the foundation of UNESCO's precursor, the International Committee for Intellectual Collaboration (IICI) of the League of Nations in 1922. While previous meetings mostly had employed internationalism to promote heritage, the League now explicitly used "the protection of cultural heritage as a tool in the promotion of internationalism." To "counter purely nationalist interest, the League fostered the notion of common cultural heritage."[35] The belief in a common heritage of humanity, and in its peacekeeping effect, prevailed also after the Second World War ended this "International" again and still animates UNESCO's mission. Between the League and the United Nations, one could again locate a "3 1/2 International" in the shape of the "Monuments Men" and other efforts to prevent the loss of cultural heritage during the war. Although the institutional framework has stayed the same after 1946, in many ways a Fifth International began gradually through the "Winds of Change" in the 1960s and the slow, but effective challenges to Western-centric ideas of heritage from within UNESCO.

The formation, and demise, of successive "Heritage Internationals" seems thus most clearly driven by major shifts in international relations. Yet more complex, and sometimes more counterintuitive, patterns also underpinned exchanges. Although the periodization suggested is useful to draw attention

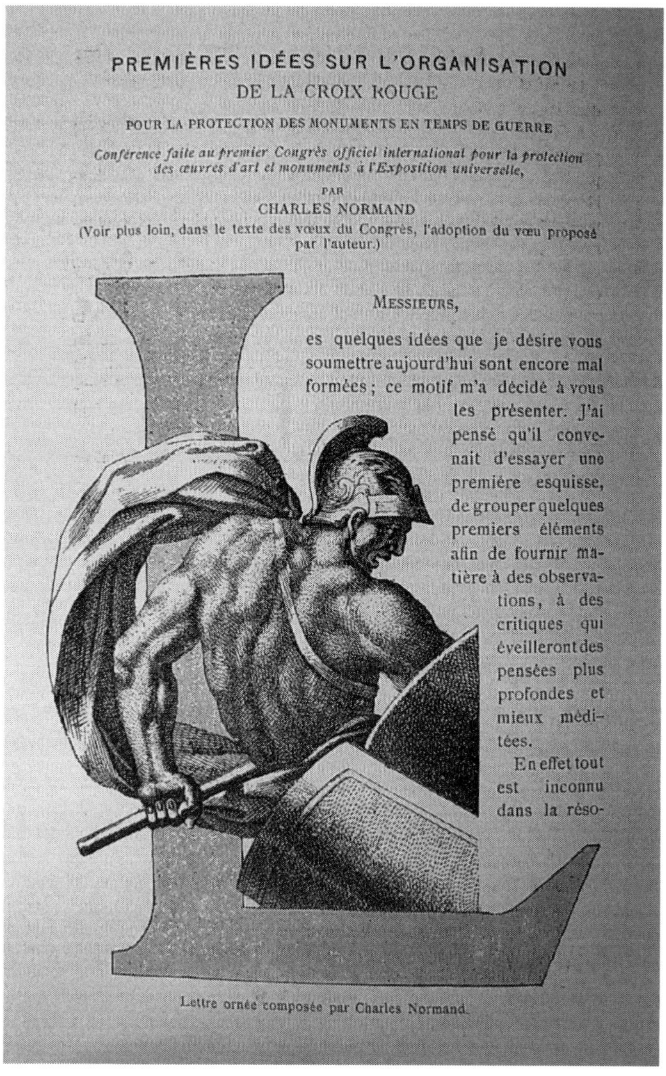

PREMIÈRES IDÉES SUR L'ORGANISATION
DE LA CROIX ROUGE

POUR LA PROTECTION DES MONUMENTS EN TEMPS DE GUERRE

Conférence faite au premier Congrès officiel international pour la protection
des œuvres d'art et monuments à l'Exposition universelle,

PAR

CHARLES NORMAND

(Voir plus loin, dans le texte des vœux du Congrès, l'adoption du vœu proposé
par l'auteur.)

MESSIEURS,

es quelques idées que je désire vous
soumettre aujourd'hui sont encore mal
formées ; ce motif m'a décidé à vous
les présenter. J'ai
pensé qu'il conve-
nait d'essayer une
première esquisse,
de grouper quelques
premiers éléments
afin de fournir ma-
tière à des observa-
tions, à des
critiques qui
éveilleront des
pensées plus
profondes et
mieux médi-
tées.
En effet tout
est inconnu
dans la réso-

Lettre ornée composée par Charles Normand.

to the repeated revival and challenge of internationalist ideas,
it risks masking the substantial continuities that persisted
across wars. Considerably more research is needed to understand to which extended wars (in particular the major multilateral conflicts) did indeed disrupt heritage internationalism
or whether they should rather be understood as crucial for the
formation of new international networks that came to fruition
once peace was restored. Moreover, these "Heritage Internationals" are not the only international ways to think about the
internationalization of heritage. On the contrary, at any given
moment, multiple heritage networks existed in parallel and
overlapping forms. Rather than ordering them through their
attitude toward internationalism as a principle, one can also
think about them in terms of membership, agenda, geography,
or materiality.

There were first of all a multitude of "Internationals of
Agents" — multilateral networks led by different state bu-

reaucracies, diplomats, cities, professions, and leisure- or interest-driven associations. None of these networks of agents operated in isolation, but they often formed distinct epistemic communities. Many used their international connections overtly to establish themselves nationally, but there were also a range of secret and clandestine networks, not only for the sake of diplomacy but also to foster the interests of dealers and buyers, and often of looters and forgers. Cutting across these communities, however, were what might be termed "Internationals of Concerns." The protection of buildings, nature, peoples, or traditions, for instance, all had their own "internationals." They repeatedly came together before being driven apart by growing professionalization. Some internationals of concerns were crisis driven (by destruction, exportation, theft, and so on); other were motivated by the desire to create institutions such as museums or parks, or to modernize planning or sanitation. At some moments, it is relatively easy to find connections between different networks, for example through the attendance lists of international congresses, but much more work needs to be done to understand when different heritage concerns coalesced and when they did not.[36]

Another way to think about internationals is through "Internationals of Spaces." Here, membership was determined in part geopolitically and in part through the imagination. Ideas about the international, the civilized, the imperial, the linguistic, or the regional shaped who was allowed in. This in turn fostered the emergence and enhancement of such ideas. There were clearly crossovers between networks that self-defined as "international,"[37] and those that saw themselves more as "Anglophone,"[38] or "British imperial,"[39] however, it is not clear yet which spaces had the closest links and where connections cut across these imagined communities.

In part this could be achieved by paying more attention to the "Internationals of Things"—and those of flora, fauna and human beings. These "internationals" were generally not as consciously self-defined as the others but are perhaps the most pervasive as a multitude of objects, specimens, and beings created their own webs: sometimes by moving around the globe, sometimes by becoming heritage in situ through the flow of international visitors, and by being appropriated intangibly in far flung corners of the earth through the imagination.[40] And then there are last but not least all the "Hidden Internationals" of knowledge exchanges, which took place in the wake of exploration, expansion, and colonization. Their acknowledgment fluctuated over time, was rarely done in full, and was often erased completely from the official record, yet they fundamentally shaped ideas of heritage from the "periphery." It is their history that offers way to decentralize and provincialize the histories of the "internationals" with which this section began.[41]

Oppression, Collaboration, and Subversion

Heritage internationalism is thus best understood as "the network of networks."[42] It is too early yet for substantial conclusions about its precise nature, but from existing studies one might extrapolate a range of factors that determined where thick connections were established. Particularly close links often drew on older, early modern, social, cultural, political, and economic ties, and their transformation mapped often neatly onto the transformation of geopolitical, diplomatic, and economic relations.[43] But new connections were also issue driven. As a result, the global networks connecting nature preservationists were much more oriented toward the Americas, Africa, and Australasia than those of cultural preservationists, but here, too, different foci existed. Those championing historic preservation, for instance, had stronger leanings toward the lands of classical antiquity that had started to protect their monuments early on, while those focusing on prehistory had closer ties toward Northern Europe, as the field was shaped in Scandinavia.[44]

How relationships were conceptualized within networks depended often on the diplomatic standing of a given country, however; modes of self-fashioning were highly contextual. The international sphere was as much used to display superiority as to mend perceived inferiorities. Before turning to an analysis of these diplomatic uses, it is, however, important to remember that (a) a large proportion of international exchanges did not primarily have political uses and that (b) many exchanges that did primarily served to improve a local or national situation. "Legitimizing one's own actions or criticizing those of others in a national debate was one incentive" for cultural transfer, while "trying to find a way out of an internal political impasse by having recourse to foreign examples was another."[45] At the same time, imitating, and surpassing, foreign heritage practices was motivated by the wish to improve one's own status and prestige internationally. Not only the possession of heritage (often achieved through plunder in distant lands) but also its preservation became increasingly a symbol of national advancement and hence part of the civilizing mission.[46] A large part of the international exchanges that existed was therefore exchanges of an unequal nature marked by physical and conceptual dispossessions and even genocide.[47] Not every case of contact should therefore be taken as evidence of a "shared" heritage history, but the hierarchies and exclusions that existed within the global networks in terms of race (as well as in terms of class and gender) need careful observation.[48]

However, as has been increasingly pointed out in the literature on colonialism and culture, hegemony is an insufficient framework for understanding what were often more complex processes of interaction.[49] Without downplaying the atrocities of imperialism, and the role played by heritage concepts in assisting in these, it is also worth noticing how often discourses and practices were subverted. The colonized often watched the colonial authorities closely to use their behavior to attack their laws, as Indra Sengupta's analysis of the preservation of religious structures in India has highlighted. In the very early twentieth century, indigenous groups employed colonial ideas of heritage to strengthen their own interests and impose limits to colonial authority, for instance by using the clauses on religious monuments in the Ancient Monuments Act for India of 1904. By appropriating the universalist language of history and aesthetics developed in the West, and by combining it with an appeal to local religious traditions, they not only obtained funding for maintenance from the colonial government but at the same time regulated and restricted British access to Indian temples and mosques.[50]

Complex, multiple, and subversive uses were not limited to the "periphery" but were equally brought to the "center," as can be illustrated through Cologne Cathedral (Figure 5). Its completion between 1840 and 1880 as *the* German national monument often serves as the textbook case for the importance of buildings for nationalism and vice-versa. However, the cathedral completion also was an international project, to which private individuals from Denmark to Mexico gave donations, and an important ploy in the diplomacy of several Western and non-Western states. The Prussian monarchy systematically brought foreign officials and heads of states to the city on the occasion of cathedral festivals and state visits. European royals were at the center of these diplomatic ceremonies in the 1840s,[51] but from the 1860s, Prussia's increasingly global ambitions became apparent in the visitors brought to see Cologne. The first Japanese delegation to visit Europe was asked by the Foreign office to stop at Cologne on the way to Berlin to visit the cathedral. The diary entries of the delegation's members reveal some bafflement at the temple they were asked to see,[52] but their visit, like later ones by an Ottoman Sultan and a Persian Shah, also show that the diplomatic uses were two-way processes. While it allowed Prussia to create diplomatic relations beyond the fields already occupied by the great imperial powers, it offered the representatives of old countries threatened by Western imperialism to establish themselves among the ranks of "civilized" partners.[53] Finally, the diplomatic attention was also used locally. The inhabitants of the city (who, even fifty years after the Rhineland had

5. Cologne Cathedral. "Projection of the Completed Cathedral," Supplement to the *Illustrated London News*, 27 MY 1843: 371. Public domain.

been given to Prussia, still perceived Prussian rule as a form of occupation) seized the diplomatic importance of these visits to comment on the cathedral project in the matter of Montesquieu's *Persian Letters*. On the occasion of the Ottoman Sultan's visit in 1867, for instance, they circumvented censorship by serializing a fake diary of the Sultan, which criticized the cathedral project as too nationalist and too conservative.[54]

In parallel to the domestic and diplomatic uses of heritage, finally, an often truly collaborative world existed. Private letters between preservationists from different countries were marked by affection even in times of war and preservationists sincerely exchanged ideas to assist each other to save heritages across national borders, and fought to establish common standards. With the wisdom of hindsight we can tell that international exchanges did not lead to peace among nations, nor did the international conventions established toward the end of the nineteenth century prevent the destruction of cultural heritage in the violent conflicts of the twentieth century. Yet it is too easy to be cynical about the instrumental nature of the belief in a common heritage of humanity—a belief that survived conflict resiliently and that nourished hopes to shape international relations peacefully. While the history of heritage internationalism has certainly too often be told as a Whig history of a continuous improvement toward universalism, a Foucauldian history of Western control goes too much the other way. Neither does the historic record justice. From a long historic perspective, heritage internationalism appears more complex, fluctuating, and multicentered. It was often as much a bottom-up process as it was a top-down one, and if we truly want to understand it, it is necessary to pay due attention to the strength of individual agency against forms of dominant discourse.

Biography
Astrid Swenson is senior lecturer in European History at Brunel University London. She is author of *The Rise of Heritage: Preserving the Past in France, Germany and England* (2013) and coeditor (with Peter Mandler) *From Plunder to Preservation: Britain and the Heritage of Empire* (2013).

Notes
My thanks to the participants of the "Heritage Diplomacy" panel at the International Association for Critical Heritage Studies' Congress in Canberra, where this paper was presented, and to Tim Winter, Bianca Gaudenzi, and the editors at *Future Anterior* for their comments on the articles.
[1] Paul Betts and Corey Ross, "Modern Historical Preservation—Towards a Global Perspective," *Past & Present* 226, no. 10 (2015): 7–26.
[2] For innovative recent approaches see, for instance, Glenda Sluga, "Editorial—The Transnational History of International Institutions," *Journal of Global History* 6 (2011): 219–22; Isabelle Anatole-Gabriel Vinson, *Essai d'histoire Intellectuelle et Politique du Patrimoine International 1945–1992* (PhD diss., EHESS Paris, 2013); Poul Duedahl, ed., *The History of UNESCO: Global Actions and Impacts* (London: Palgrave Macmillan, forthcoming); Christoph Brumann and David Berliner, eds., *World Heritage on the Ground: Ethnographic Perspectives* (Oxford, U.K.: Berghan, forthcoming).
[3] Jean-François Sirinelli, Commentary to "The Making of Histories of International Organizations: UNESCO as a Case Study," *22nd International Congress of Historical Sciences*, Jinan, August 28, 2015.
[4] Tim Winter, "Heritage Diplomacy," http://conferences.criticalheritagestudies.org/sites/default/files/ID53%20Heritage%20Diplomacy.docx; Tim Winter "Heritage Diplomacy," *International Journal of Heritage Studies* 5 (2015): 997–1015. (All reference below to Winter, "Heritage Diplomacy," are to this *IJHS* article).
[5] UNESCO, "About Us," http://portal.unesco.org/en/ev.php-URL_ID=3328&URL_DO=DO_TOPIC&URL_SECTION=201.html; Akira Iriye, *Cultural Internationalism and World Order* (Baltimore: John Hopkins University Press, 1997).
[6] Astrid Swenson, *The Rise of Heritage: Preserving the Past in France, Germany, and England, 1789–1914* (Cambridge: Cambridge University Press, 2013).
[7] Laurajane Smith, *Uses of Heritage* (London: Routledge, 2006).
[8] Astrid Swenson and Peter Mandler, eds., *From Plunder to Preservation: Britain and the Heritage of Empire, 1800–1950* (Oxford: Proceedings of the British Academy 187, 2013).
[9] Christopher Alan Bayly, *The Birth of the Modern World, 1780–1914: Global Connections and Comparisons* (Oxford: Blackwell, 2004); Jürgen Osterhammel and

Niels P Petersson, *Geschichte der Globalisierung: Dimensionen, Prozesse, Epochen* (Munich: CH Beck, 2003); Jürgen Osterhammel, *Die Verwandlung der Welt: Eine Geschichte des 19. Jahrhunderts* (Munich: CH Beck, 2010).

10 On the idea of an "authorized" heritage discourse, see Smith, *Uses of Heritage*.

11 See, more broadly, Sunil Amrith and Glenda Sluga, "New Histories of the United Nations," *Journal of World History* 19, no. 3 (2008): 251–74.

12 On the difficulties of projecting back terminology and on the semantic development of the heritage concept, see Astrid Swenson, "'Heritage,' 'Patrimoine,' und 'Kulturerbe': Eine vergleichende historische Semantik," in *Prädikat 'Heritage': Wertschoepfung aus kulturellen Resourcen*, eds,. Dorothee Hemme, Markus Tauschek and Regina Bendix, 53–74 (Münster: LIT Verlag, 2007); Nabila Oulebsir and Astrid Swenson, "Patrimoine: voyages des mots. Heritage, Erbe, Beni culturali, Turâth, Tigemmi," *Patrimoine et Architecture* (2015): 10–23 at 21–22.

13 John Henry Merryman, "Cultural Property Internationalism," *International Journal of Cultural Property* 12 (2005): 11–39; Roger O'Keefe, *The Protection of Cultural Property in Armed Conflict* (Cambridge: Cambridge University Press, 2006); Jukka Jokilehto, *History of Architectural Conservation* (London: Routledge, 2007).

14 Melanie Hall, ed., *Towards World Heritage: International Origins of the Preservation Movement* (Aldershot, U.K.: Ashgate, 2011); Anna-Katharina Wöbse, *Weltnaturschutz: Umweltdiplomatie in Völkerbund und Vereinten Nationen 1920–1950* (Frankfurt: Campus, 2012); Swenson, *Rise of Heritage*; Swenson and Mandler, eds., *From Plunder to Preservation*; Ian Tyrrell, "America's National Parks: The Transnational Creation of National Space in the Progressive Era," *Journal of American Studies* 46, no. 1 (2012): 1–21; Michael Falser and Monica Juneja, eds., *Kulturerbe und Denkmalpflege transkulturell: Grenzgänge zwischen Theorie und Praxis* (Bielefeld: Transcript Verlag, 2014); Andrea Meyer and Benedicte Savoy, eds., *The Museum Is Open: Towards a Transnational History of Museums 1750–1940* (Berlin: de Gruyter, 2014); Paul Betts and Corey Ross, eds., *Heritage in the Modern World: Past & Present* 226, no. 10 (2015). In addition to these globally focused studies, there exists a growing range of in-depth historical studies that reveal the density of exchanges in particular regions. The following discussion draws in particular on Bénédicte Savoy, *Patrimoine annexé: Les biens culturels saisis par la France en Allemagne autour de 1800* (2 vols.; Paris: MSH, 2003); Nabila Oulebsir, *Les Usages du patrimoine. Monuments, musées et politiques coloniale en Algérie 1830–1930* (Paris: MSH, 2004); Holger Hoock, *Empires of the Imagination: Politics, War, and the Arts in the British World, 1750–1850* (London: Profile Books, 2010); Sujit Sivasundaram, *Islanded: Britain, Sri Lanka, and the Bounds of an Indian Ocean Colony* (Chicago: University of Chicago Press, 2013); Stefanie Gänger, *Relics of the Past: The Collecting and Study of Pre-Columbian Antiquities in Peru and Chile, 1837–1911* (Oxford: Oxford University Press, 2014).

15 For a more extended discussion, see Swenson, *Rise of Heritage*, 1–21.

16 For two advocacies of broad understandings, see Michael Werner and Bénédicte Zimmermann, "Beyond Comparison: Histoire Croisee and the Challenge of Reflexibity," *History and Theory*, 45, no. 1 (2006): 30–50, and Ian Tyrrell, "Reflections on the Transnational Turn in United States History: Theory and Practice," *Journal of Global Histor*, 4, no. 3 (2009): 453–74. On recent debates, see Kiran Klaus Patel, "An Emperor without Clothes? The Debate about Transnational History Twenty-five Years On," *Histoire@Politique* 26 (2015): www.histoire-politique.fr.

17 A transnational framework makes for instance sense when looking at entities that understood themselves as nations, but less for so for understanding for instance imperial networks, see Tamson Pietsch, *Empire of Scholars: Universities, Networks, and the British Academic World, 1850–1939* (Manchester, U.K.: Manchester University Press, 2013).

18 Swenson, *Rise of Heritage*, 20.

19 Winter, "Heritage Diplomacy," 1006.

20 Ibid., 11.

21 Annie Kriegel, *Les Internationales Ouvrières (1864–1943)* (Paris: Presses universitaires de France, 1964).

22 Abigail Green and Vincent Viaene, "Introduction: Rethinking Religion and Globalization," in *Religious Internationals in the Modern World: Globalization and Faith Communities since 1750*, ed. Abigail Green and Vincent Viaene, 1–9 (London: Palgrave MacMillan 2012).

23 On broader patterns, see Martin H. Geyer and Johannes Paulmann, eds., *The Mechanics of Internationalism: Culture, Society, and Politics from the 1840s to the First World War* (Oxford: Oxford University Press, 2001), and Glenda Sluga, *Internationalism in the Age of Nationalism* (Philadelphia: Pennsylvania University Press, 2013).

24 See, for instance, Jokilehto, *History of Architectural Conservation*; Margaret M. Miles, *Art as Plunder: The Ancient Origins of Debate about Cultural Property* (Cambridge: Cambridge University Press, 2008).

25 Winter, "Heritage Diplomacy," 1000.

26 Swenson, *Rise of Heritage*, ch. 1.

27 On this periodization, see Swenson, *Rise of Heritage,* 336.

28 Antoine-Chrysostome Quatremère de Quincy, *Lettres à Miranda sur le Déplacement des Monuments de L'art de L'Italie,* ed. Eduard Pommier (Paris: Macula, 1989), 88.

29 Savoy, *Patrimoine Annexé.*

30 Hall, ed., *Towards World Heritage*; Swenson, *Rise of Heritage,* ch. 2 and 4.

31 Alan Kramer, *Dynamic of Destruction: Culture and Mass Killing in the First World War* (Oxford: Oxford University Press, 2007).

32 Christina Kott, *Préserver l'art de l'ennemi?: le Patrimoine Artistique en Belgique et en France Occupées, 1914–1918* (Bruxelles: Peter Lang, 2006).

33 Institut International de Coopération intellectuelle, Office international des Musées, *La Protection internationale des monuments historique et des œuvres d'art en temps de guerre* (Paris: n.p., 1936), 12, UNESCO Archives, Paris, IICI/14/9.

34 Kriegel, *Les Internationales Ouvrières.*

35 S. M. Titchen, *On the Construction of Outstanding Universal Value: UNESCO's World Heritage Convention (Convention Concerning the Protection of the World Cultural and Natural Heritage, 1972) and the Identification and Assessment of Cultural Places for the Inclusion in the World Heritage List* (PhD diss.; Canberra: Australian National University, 1995), 14.

36 Swenson, *Rise of Heritage,* ch. 4.

37 Ibid.

38 Melanie Hall, "Niagara Falls: Preservation and the Spectacle of Anglo-American Accord," in *Towards World Heritage,* ed. Hall, 23–43.

39 Astrid Swenson, "The Heritage of Empire,", in *From Plunder to Preservation,* eds. Swenson and Mandler, 3–28; Paul Basu and Vinita Damodaran, "Colonial Histories of Heritage: Legislative Migrations and the Politics of Preservation," *Past & Present* 226, no. 10 (2015): 240–71.

40 Neil MacGregor, *A History of the World in a Hundred Objects* (London: Allen Lane, 2010); Peter Coates, "Creatures Enshrined: Wild Animals as Bearers of Heritage," *Past & Present* 226, no. 10 (2015): 272–98; Sadiah Qureshi, *Peoples on Parade: Exhibitions, Empire and Anthropology in Nineteenth-Century Britain* (Chicago: University of Chicago Press, 2011).

41 Felix Driver and L. Jones, *Hidden Histories of Exploration: Researching the RGS-IBG Collections* (London: Royal Geographic Society, 2009); Felix Driver, "Hidden Histories Made Visible? Reflections on a Geographical Exhibition," *Transactions of the Institute of British Geographers* 38, no. 3 (2013): 420–35; Sivasundaram Sujit, "Appropriation to Supremacy: Ideas of the 'Native' in the Rise of British Imperial Heritage," in *From Plunder to Preservation,* eds. Swenson and Mandler, 149–70; Dipesh Chakrabarty, *Provincializing Europe: Postcolonial Thought and Historical Difference: Postcolonial Thought and Historical Difference* (Princeton, N.J.: Princeton University Press, 2009).

42 Winter, "Heritage Diplomacy," 998.

43 Astrid Swenson, "Cologne Cathedral as an International Monument," in *Rewriting German History,* eds. Jan Rüger and Nikolaus Wachsmann, 29–51(London: Palgrave MacMillan, 2015).

44 Swenson, *Rise of Heritage,* 331.

45 Geyer and Paulmann, eds., *Mechanics of Internationalism,*16.

46 Swenson, "The Heritage of Empire," 3–28; Michael Falser, ed., *Cultural Heritage as Civilizing Mission: From Decay to Recovery* (Cham: Springer, 2015).

47 Sadiah Qureshi, "Dying Americans: Race, Extinction, and Conservation in the New World," in *From Plunder to Preservation,* eds. Swenson and Mandler, 267–86.

48 On the gendering of preservationist networks see Astrid Swenson, "'To every landless man, woman and child in England': Octavia Hill and the preservation movement", in *Nobler imaginings and mightier struggles: Octavia Hill and the remaking of British society,* eds. Elizabeth Baignet and Ben Cowell (London: Institute for Historical Research 2016): 187-208.

49 Londa Schiebinger, "Forum Introduction: The European Colonial Science Complex," *Isis* 96, no. 1 (2005): 52–55.

50 Indra Sengupta, "Monument Preservation and the Vexing Question of Religious Structures in Colonial India," in *From Plunder to Preservation,* eds. Swenson and Mandler, 171–85.

51 E.g. "Her Majesty's Visit to Germany," *The Times,* August 22, 1845, 5.

52 Rolf-Harald Wippich, "Nicht alltägliche Besucher—die japanische Europagesandtschaft im Kölner Dom im Sommer 1862," *Kölner Domblatt* (2013): 271–9

53 David Motadel, "Qajar Shahs in Imperial Germany," *Past & Present* 213, no. 1 (2011): 191–235

54 Beate Dorfey and Mario Kramp, "Der Sultan, das Rheinland under Kölner Dom. Eine historische Posse aus dem Jahr 1867," *Kölner Domblatt* (2006): 185–204.

1. Skyline of Sana'a, Yemen. Photograph by the author.

Tim Winter

Heritage Diplomacy
Entangled Materialities of International Relations

Future Anterior
Volume XIII, Number 1
Summer 2016

This article explores both the history and future of international preservation through the concept of heritage diplomacy. In the limited space of an article, the aim is not to be comprehensive but rather open up some themes and analytical threads that have hitherto received much less attention than they deserve. Indeed, the thrust for exploring heritage diplomacy emerges from a sense that there are some significant gaps in scholarship, ones that can best be filled by bringing the insights of a number of disciplines together. Interestingly, scholars working under the banner of international relations or political science have paid little attention to the material world, let alone to the role material culture has played in diplomacy and international affairs in the modern era. Equally, the fields of preservation and heritage studies have made only rare and tentative forays into theories of governance or globalization. As a consequence, while much has been written about the history of preservation and its internationalization, scholarship has been oriented around a limited repertoire of conceptual and empirical frames. Foremost here is the nation-state, with numerous books and PhD dissertations dedicated to tracing histories of preservation in the United States, Sweden, Italy, or offering comparative analyses of the heritage traditions of France and England, for example.[1] In such cases, national boundaries have represented both the empirical and conceptual frontiers of study. While geographically more expansive, accounts of heritage and preservation within the contexts of empire and colonialism have also largely been cast within the framework of nations and territories. For those attempting to understand the global ordering of preservation in late modernity, organizations like UNESCO have often provided the point of focus with critical discourse analyses of their policies and programs remaining a popular approach. Indeed with UNESCO and others having become metonyms for the globalization of heritage and governance of culture, considerable attention has been given to understanding—and deconstructing—international treaties, declarations, and charters and to the implications they have for on the ground policies. While these various approaches and framings undoubtedly provide crucial and highly instructive insights, my aim here is to point toward some alternative points of analytical departure, ones that bring into focus elements of preservation that evade scrutiny within these frameworks and

approaches, and yet bear upon both the history and future of
heritage preservation in critical ways.

Elsewhere, I have explored heritage diplomacy in both historical and conceptual terms to illustrate how preservation has
been inherently tied to the rise of internationalism and those
structures of international relations and global governance that
emerged in the modern era.[2] It is an argument that sees each
as part of the story of the other. Indeed, one of the defining
features of our contemporary, interconnected world has been
the rapid expansion of the international governance of culture,
including the safeguarding of those cultural remnants from the
past. In the domain of heritage preservation, notable examples
include the emergence of such institutions as The Getty Conservation Institute, Aga Khan Trust For Culture, World Monuments
Fund, Global Heritage Fund, as well as those bodies known
primarily around the world by their acronyms: UNESCO, ICOM,
ICCROM, and ICOMOS.[3] We have also seen a major expansion
in the number of nongovernmental bodies and foundations
using heritage preservation as a mechanism for advancing
their core goals, many of which may not be directly related
to the cultural sector. Examples here include The Henry Luce
Foundation, The Asia Foundation, and The Lee Foundation.
Accompanying much of this activity has been the vast growth
in philanthropic funding, which has permeated numerous sectors of international discourse, including that of preservation.
The United States has developed an influential and somewhat
unique tradition of private, philanthropic aid supporting the
cultural sector internationally. With tax incentives enabling an
inflow of funds to heritage-related initiatives, support has often
been characterized by the personal causes and interests of
individual donors.

To further pursue such lines of enquiry here, the discussion centers around three key themes: venues, cooperation,
and borders. These are far from comprehensive and are presented as launchpads in the hope that they can open up some
unfamiliar, challenging, yet fruitful lines of enquiry.

Venues

All diplomacy needs its venues, whether it be meeting rooms in
Geneva and New York or the Mount Washington Hotel infamous
for hosting the Bretton Woods Conference of 1944. Heritage
diplomacy is no exception, and by citing a number of indicative examples, the discussion here explores why certain places
become venues of cooperation and preservation at very specific moments in history. As authors such as Swenson, Reid,
and others have shown, the crossing of borders and oceans
to assist with the preservation of the cultural past has a long
history.[4] Eras of exploration and subsequent structures of

colonialism established a host of networks, institutions, and bilateral relations, and as Swenson notes in her essay in this issue, histories of preservation in such contexts need to be read in relation to the ascendancy of an ethos of internationalism. To complement this insight, my initial focus here is the 1950s, a hugely formative but often overlooked period. The reconstruction of global peace and economic stability after World War II, combined with decolonization and the emergent Cold War, heralded a new era of international cooperation, geopolitical alignments, and bilateral arrangements. It was within this environment that the international landscape of heritage governance we recognize today took shape.

As William Carruthers suggests in his article in this special issue, the Abu Simbel campaign of the late 1950s and after is widely celebrated as an iconic and formative moment of international cooperation, one that would provide the template for the World Heritage movement that followed in the 1970s. Less emphasized, though, is the political context, both domestic and international, that enabled it. In many ways Egypt—as a North African developing country emerging from quasi-colonial rule at one of the geographic crossroads of the Cold War—was uniquely placed to receive multilateral assistance. Egypt had also been host to numerous archaeological teams from European countries from the late nineteenth century onwards, and unlike newly independent countries such as India or Morocco, it was not as bound by the bilateral ties that were maintained for those countries in the decades after independence. But as Allias notes, various diplomatic obstacles needed to be overcome in the aftermath of the Suez Crisis and the freezing of relations with former colonial powers before international cooperation could go ahead.[5] With the Soviet Union providing financial assistance for constructing the dam that would lead to the flooding of the valley further south, Abu Simbel presented a number of Western allies the opportunity to assemble for a diplomatically expedient initiative, a project UNESCO has subsequently described as a "triumph of international solidarity."[6] The internationalism of preservation, based around an ethos of multilateral cooperation and scientistic materialism thus required venues with certain political and geographic qualities. Accordingly, campaigns to "save" Venice and the archaeological sites of Borobudur in Indonesia and Moehenjodaro in Pakistan all emerged within particular sociopolitical contexts and/or in the wake of catastrophic events such as wars or earthquakes. The case of Angkor in Cambodia is particularly illustrative of this point. The arrival of multilateral preservation aid occurred on the back of a prolonged period of civil war and economic underdevelopment. Crucially, however, it also depended on a series of domestic political transitions

2. Abu Simbel Monument, Egypt. Photograph by the author.

3. Srinagar, Kashmir. Photograph by the author.

and reforms, namely the 1991 Paris Peace Accords and UN-sponsored elections.[7] Parallels can be seen in Myanmar today. Reforms in 2010 triggered a wave of international assistance programs for the city of Yangon and the country's key archaeological sites. Given that Myanmar appears committed to a path of "opening up," it is highly likely a flourishing heritage diplomacy sector will emerge in the wake of Aung San Suu Kyi's victory in the landmark elections of November 2015. The timing and presence of international collaborations to preserve heritage in places such as Cambodia and Myanmar has thus been contingent upon a convergence of very specific factors.

The point to note here, then, is that a key factor shaping the internationalization of preservation has been where and when heritage diplomacy—whether it be via bilateral or multilateral structures—comes to be assembled. In comprehending this we need to look at the presence of certain geopolitical forces and their intersection with transitions in the political environment of a country, or the presence of historically significant moments such as elections or natural disasters. Interpersonal networks and connections, together with much larger cultural or historic bonds, as we shall see shortly, are also critical in determining which places or causes receive support. By implication then, by critically reading such factors as key determinants in the activation of international preservation projects, we can also develop an interpretive frame for understanding why certain places fail to emerge as sites of cooperation and assistance. During the Cold War, Egypt and South Asia were priority aid countries for a number of Western countries. Equally, Moscow funded archaeology and preservation within the spheres of influence of the Soviet Union. Today, bilateral preservation agreements between countries invariably align with the strategic foreign policy goals of the donor.

As a result, historically significant sites such as Sana'a in Yemen or Srinagar in Indian-administered Kashmir (see Figures 1 and 3) are just two examples of places that either fall outside these logics or are encased by local political conditions that provide significant barriers to international cooperation. The case of Angkor is also indicative of the importance of the cultural politics of the host state in determining the likelihood of a site emerging as a venue of preservation collaboration. For the Cambodian government, the restoration of Angkor powerfully stood as a metaphor for a cultural, national, and ethnic revival. Millions of dollars of aid in preservation assistance and the attention lauded upon Angkor provided the state with considerable prestige on the international stage, as well as GDP-significant income from tourism.[8] Such an example lies in distinct contrast to the dynamics surrounding support for the heritage preservation of minority groups, which can vary greatly from country to country.

As the international heritage preservation movement has expanded its focus beyond sites of antiquity we have seen the numbers and types of sites receiving assistance proliferate. Greater focus has been given to preserving those sites and structures with challenging or contentious legacies, as well as built environments of more recent times. Notwithstanding this growing diversity, some patterns remain in place, with venues of collaboration and heritage diplomacy typically emerging as such due to their relative neutrality within a domestic or regional context, expediency in larger international affairs, or because they represent a positive focal point for aid and assistance programs conducted in postwar or disaster-reconstruction contexts. Indeed the restoration of built heritage has become a powerful symbol and metaphor for reconstruction or reconciliation in recent times, as examples such as the Mostar Bridge or mosques in Banda Aceh testify. Naturally, the greater the alignment between these different factors, the more likely it is that the scale and scope of preservation aid will expand. Looking beyond venues of international assistance and collaboration, other historically significant sites and buildings have also come to possess diplomatic value through their preservation. The Hiroshima Peace Memorial Park, for example, with its internationally iconic A-Bomb Dome has helped Japan project a desire for peace as a narrative on the international stage in the aftermath of World War II. Likewise, Auschwitz, Robben Island, or the Kigali Genocide Memorial in Rwanda have all played a similar role in image projection.

4. Temple Preservation at Bagan, Myanmar funded by Buddhist Association, South Korea. Photograph by the author.

Many more examples could be cited, but the assertion made here centers around the value of understanding why preservation activity and funding arrives in certain places and at particular moments, and the ways in which this has shaped the heritage-preservation movement and its internationalization in modern times. To draw on the terminology of actor-network theory, it is an analytical path that reveals the role cultural heritage and material culture play as nonhuman actors in modern diplomatic relations. Material culture thus possesses its own agency, both enabling and responding to specific forms of international relations and alignments, and, in so doing, giving structure to modes of cooperation. Assemblages form around cultural heritage, whereby at certain moments we see institutions, expertise, finance, and technologies come together to constitute and enact the ethos of preservation.[9]

Cooperation

An implicit yet vital ingredient to the above discussion is cooperation. It is a language that needs a careful unpacking, as it collapses and conceals those imbalances and asymmetries of power and resources that are almost always built into relationships between agencies, individuals, or countries. With the modern international heritage preservation sector structured around a benign nomenclature of partnerships and collaborations, subtle forms of exploitation, subversive power, or the unanticipated capacities for sovereignty that aid often affords invariably remain hidden within notions of equanimity and equivalence.

Wars, and the need for reconstruction and reconciliation in their aftermath, have long been a key driver of international preservation efforts. As Beyen and Cortjaens both document, German architects and guilds developed campaigns to redevelop and rebuild Belgium's cities and historic buildings during and after the First World War.[10] The widespread destruction inflicted upon Europe's cities during World War II would however demand a new scale of reconstruction and assistance. The scale of the conflict, together with the era of decolonization that ensued, fostered a new infrastructure of multilateralism. In effect then, through the establishment of UNESCO, ICCROM, and ICOM, we see the creation of new platforms and forums of internationalism from which a complex, networked structure of heritage cooperation and diplomacy could emerge. It is an infrastructure that continues to function today, wherein such international agencies and intergovernmental bodies interact and cofund initiatives with states and nongovernmental institutions around the world.

As noted earlier, recent decades have seen a rapid proliferation of the number of actors involved in the cultural sector. The growth of nongovernmental organizations in the global governance landscape since the early 1990s has led to a situation whereby heritage preservation is enmeshed in a network of networks. Conflicts in the Balkans and Iraq also led to an increased prominence given to the reconstruction of cultural heritage and built environments by the international humanitarian aid sector. In 2015 the international attention for cultural heritage reached new heights as media outlets such as CNN, *The Guardian,* or *The New York Times* presented countless stories and images of heritage destruction and damage in their coverage of ISIS and the civil war in Syria or the major earthquakes suffered by Nepal and Afghanistan.

Despite this proliferation of actors and the internationally high profile of UNESCO, for many countries the state continues to play a key role in the international preservation scene. Bilateral aid continues to be a defining feature of today's global heritage—development nexus. As Natsuko Akagawa demonstrates in this issue, Japan has folded its heritage conservation aid within its wider foreign policy goals and strategies since the decades following World War II. But as she notes, cultural aid has been more than merely an appendage to those "harder" forms of economic and developmental aid. For Japan, as with the other countries in its region, heritage diplomacy represents

5. Temple Preservation at Bagan, Myanmar funded by Buddhist Association, South Korea. Photograph by the author.

a valuable space for advancing deeper cultural and historical narratives. Through collaborations and heritage aid packages in countries such as Afghanistan, Bangladesh, Cambodia, India, Laos, Mongolia, Myanmar, Nepal, and Pakistan, Japan has been able to connect and revivify the cultural, religious, and historical ties it shares with the wider Asian continent. In other words, the geographies of this modern heritage cooperation can be mapped onto those cultural flows and connections of a much deeper history. To return to Myanmar, an exploration of such themes reveals how proposed collaborations around heritage preservation in recent years speak to the country's location as the "crossroads" of two great civilizations. As India and China compete for economic and political influence in their region, heritage-preservation collaborations enable some very specific narratives of nation and history to be advanced. As it became more apparent that the shift toward a civilian government would be accompanied by the opening up of Myanmar's economy, both India and China advanced their trade and assistance packages. On a visit to Yangon in May 2012, Manmohan Singh, then prime minister of India, drew upon a discourse of mutual pasts and shared heritage to build trust and alliances in contemporary diplomatic relations. Accordingly, he spoke of how "India and Myanmar share age old cultural and civilizational ties. Merchants, monks and maritime traders carried influences and traditions from one to the other. . . . our common Buddhist heritage is an even stronger spiritual bond among our peoples."[11] On the back of the visit, the Archaeological

6. Post—World Heritage Listing celebrations for "Qhapaq Ñan, Andean Road System," Doha, 2014. Photograph by the author.

Survey of India offered assistance to restore a number of temples at one of Myanmar's most important historic sites, Bagan, declared to be an ancient and iconic landscape "whose architecture is similar to temples in Bengal and Orissa."[12] In a similar vein, a number of Chinese institutions have also been offering heritage conservation assistance in Myanmar since the early 2010s. But as I have argued elsewhere, these initiatives are underpinned by discourses of civilization, such that intra-regional heritage conservation aid allows both India and China to advance the idea that their "great cultures" stretched much further than the current boundaries of the nation-state.[13] In such examples we also see how cultural heritage and heritage con-servation assistance are playing an increasingly prominent role in the foreign policies of numerous non-Western and emerg-ing powers, and in their relations with countries both within and outside their respective regions. Crucially, these shifts in cultural sector aid are occurring on the back of changes in the geographies of developmental aid in regions such as Asia and the Middle East, where countries like India, Qatar, and South Korea are investing heavily in overseas aid programs.

Stepping back, it is important to tease out some of the different ways heritage diplomacy comes to be activated. To do this, we can differentiate heritage *in* diplomacy from heritage *as* diplomacy. The former highlights the various ways in which cultural heritage figures into existing diplomatic ties that have

7. World Heritage Committee meeting, Doha. Photograph by the author.

been built around trade, the bonds of colonialism, conflict, or for particular strategic reasons. Within such instances, heritage diplomacy often revolves around the forms of preservation aid noted above, whereby one country provides assistance to another: the United States to Iraq or India to Myanmar. Taking on multiple forms, this typically includes conservation and heritage-management aid, technology transfer, capacity building, or institutional support. In cases where heritage merely operates within a broader diplomatic or policy context, collaboration and forms of cooperation are not dependent on any sense of a substantive shared or mutual culture. In other instances, though, architecture, archaeological remains, traditional dance forms, food, and textiles are all being presented *as* shared heritage by former colonial powers and rising regional powers alike in the name of creating forms of historical and cultural conjoining. In the annual meetings of the World Heritage Committee, we now see committee members liberally using terms such as *flows, crossroads, cultural ties, bridges,* and *pilgrimage* to justify the inscription of sites onto the World Heritage List. Given that world heritage has become an important platform for establishing connections from the past as the basis for future cooperation, it is interesting to consider which countries are better "placed" to take advantage of such a discourse. Turkey, for example, is able to establish ties with countries right across Europe and Asia through the language of crossroads and flows in a way that, say, Canada or Norway are clearly unable to. World heritage has thus become a forum that encourages states to be internationally disposed, wherein a culture of cooperation propagates internationalized cultural nationalisms and the building of bridges through shared pasts. But as we saw in the example of India's interests in Myanmar, signaling the cultural past as a shared heritage gives significant diplomatic weight to today's bilateral relations.

Borders

Much of what I have discussed involves the crossing of international borders. Looking at this more closely, the concept of the border helps us think through how cultural heritage becomes politicized, the dynamics by which it can act as a catalyst of new political relations, and the subtle but important ways the enterprise of conserving and managing culture alters when borders are crossed. To begin this line of argument we can look to the now-familiar debates concerning the diplomatic tensions associated with the ownership of museum objects around the world. As Christine Sylvester highlights, the ongoing dispute between Britain and Greece concerning the Elgin Marbles is one of many examples of tensions that surround repatriation.[14] At the same time, we have also seen the museum emerge as an important venue of cultural diplomacy. Countries such as Mexico and Peru, for example, have invested heavily in exhibiting their cultural past through the museums of the world's major cities, forging cordial relations between institutions and peoples.

In the museum context, the crossing of borders happens through the artifact, whereas with immobile heritage other flows occur, namely those of funding, expertise, technologies, or institutionalized practices of governance. Elsewhere I have explored factors such as language, prestige, cultural knowledge (or shortfalls thereof) as factors that lead to a privileging of scientistic materialism when preservation crosses borders and involves cross-cultural encounters.[15] Without further belaboring such points, I would just suggest that the international history of heritage preservation has been one of host—guest relations, where the need to respect difference, forms of sovereignty, and avoid explicit criticism have been the keys to maintaining successful long-term projects and collaborations. Internationally operating preservation institutions have long understood this and the importance of going through "formal channels" for permissions and clearance, as well as the value of including their own embassies and ambassadors in project planning, to ensure local political and cultural systems are respected and incorporated. In diplomatic terms, for the apparatus of states, cultural assistance projects are often perceived as benign and mechanisms for constructive international engagement, with endorsements of support given to initiatives that help foster "goodwill." Even for those heritage projects that are not state funded, when operating overseas, operations remain part of a country's "cultural export" and, as such, are frequently absorbed into the bureaucratic structures of diplomacy and international relations. The John Paul Getty Trust, the Rockefeller and Luce foundations—all of which have engaged in cultural aid projects—are among those that contributed to favorable diplomatic relations and the popular appeal of the United States as it increased its global influence in the second half of the twentieth century. The implication here is that such issues not only influence the types of projects that receive political and financial support but also affect in distinct ways how they are conducted. Issues perceived to be risky or contentious, such as land use, community access, or popular religious practices, tend to receive much less support than the more science- and engineering-based activities of restoring artworks or fabric.

The twentieth century saw considerable efforts to limit and prevent the movement of material culture across national borders, with a host of international treaties, laws, and protocols drafted, signed, and ratified to achieve such goals. Equally, ever-increasing regulatory frameworks for policing national boundaries have meant lines of jurisdiction have been clearly drawn over the ownership of the cultural past. Where ambiguities linger, however, violence or diplomatic tensions can arise. One notorious example of this in recent times centered around the Preah Vihear temple, located on the border between Cambodia and Thailand. Surmounting an escarpment that marks the boundary between the two countries, Preah Vihear—or to be more precise its listing as world heritage—triggered a prolonged conflict resulting in scores of deaths. At one level, the site represented a shared heritage of temple construction and culture stretching over centuries. The nomination process, however, got caught up in the national elections of both countries, with their respective leaders using the temple to fuel the flames of nationalism and xenophobia. Further complications arose from other countries in the region quietly supporting both Thailand and Cambodia over their claims of ownership and right to manage the site's future development.

But where we see the careful policing of boundaries it is also important to recognize under what circumstances states are making borders more permeable vis-à-vis the cultural past. The process of nominating sites to the World Heritage List, for example, has long encouraged governments to be internationally disposed, requiring them to be open to various mechanisms of foreign collaboration and evaluation. Moreover, to return to the theme of cooperation, the growth of transnational and serial nominations within the world heritage system has

8. Reconstruction of Ta Prohm Temple, Angkor, Cambodia by Archaeological Survey of India, 2011. Photograph by the author.

encouraged countries to collaborate and identify links and connections that traverse their modern political frontiers. Of course countries bring their own motivations to this UN arena of cooperation, with the extraordinary One Belt, One Road project, led by China, offering a case in point. Launched in 2013, this initiative involves the development of a network of trade and investment routes that flow through Central and West Asia, and connect cities in regions as far apart as Southeast Asia and North Africa. Incorporating the Silk Road Economic Belt and 21st Century Maritime Silk Road, One Belt, One Road uses the preservation of cultural heritage as part of China's cultural diplomacy offensive within an overarching strategy of regional integration. In 2014, the first part of this initiative, the Silk Road: the Routes Network of Chang'an—Tianshan Corridor, jointly nominated by China, Kazakhstan, and Kyrgyzstan, was added to the World Heritage List. This provided a platform for future heritage preservation collaborations and subsequent nominations that will incorporate further historic settlements along the original Silk Road, as well as those port cities and shipwrecks that stand as legacies of maritime routes and trade. Such ambitions suggest that One Belt, One Road will be the largest heritage-preservation collaboration ever conceived.

Seen together, then, these various examples illustrate how borders have shaped the nature of heritage preservation in particular ways, and contributed to cooperation and contestation

9. Temple reconstruction by Archaeological Survey of India, Ta Prohm, Angkor, Cambodia, 2011. Photograph by the author.

serving as two sides of the same coin of heritage diplomacy. Preah Vihear and One Belt, One Road also illustrate the very different circumstances under which cultural heritage and the narratives surrounding preservation can, on the one hand, be linked to the strident demarcation of borders or, on the other, be closely tied to policies that actively foster transnational flows of people, capital, and goods.

Conclusion

In summary, I would suggest heritage diplomacy is a uniquely interesting phenomena, in that it speaks to deep cultural roots/routes—sometimes shared, sometimes exclusionary—and the ways these come to be filtered and appropriated through the ideologies and realpolitik of contemporary international relations, geopolitics, and nationalism. A key assertion here is that such political and economic forces have been important drivers of the modern preservation movement over the last century and a half, to a degree that is yet to be fully appreciated. The provision of state funded and nongovernmental assistance is inherently political and shaped by past and present world orders. Although it might be tempting to regard the provision of assistance in heritage preservation as an essentially apolitical activity, closer inspection reveals how donor states have long engaged in this sector as a mechanism of both soft and hard power.

I have intentionally selected examples and themes that signal some historically significant ways this international

10. Ta Prohm colonnade, reconstructed by Archaeological Survey of India, Angkor, Cambodia, 2011. Photograph by the author.

arena is now changing on the back of rapidly developing non-Western economies and a wider shift in the global order. Heritage diplomacy is thus offered in the hope that it can provide an analytical frame for making sense of these complex, multiscalar political entanglements the cultural past now finds itself caught up in. Too often academic analyses of heritage governance and preservation privilege certain actors, whether they be individuals or institutions, and cast their projects, activities, and worldviews in a social and political vacuum. I would suggest a more productive approach to understanding the complexities of international heritage preservation today lies in an analytical frame that grasps the complex dance between nationalism and internationalism that has been in place from the mid-nineteenth century onward, one that continues to orient the interactions between intergovernmental and nongovernmental agencies operating in the cultural sector and governments. The rise of IS (ISIS/ISIL/Daesh) dramatically raised the temperature on debates about cultural or religious wars. The destruction of archaeological sites, mosques, and museums in Syria and Iraq placed cultural heritage front and center in this debate. Clearly there is an urgent need for more effective responses to IS as well as analytically expansive accounts of the political and economic drivers that entangle cultural heritage in international affairs. It is hoped the themes explored here represent a helpful step in such directions.

It is widely recognized that the structures and institutions of the modern heritage-preservation movement ostensibly emanated from the West, driven by those invested in construct-

11. Ta Prohm colonnade, pre-restoration by Archaeological Survey of India, Angkor, Cambodia, 2011. Photograph by the author.

ing a liberal order and its associated forms of power. And while there is little doubt the formation of an intergovernmental landscape in the wake of World War II helped create a bureaucratic paradigm and transnational epistemic community for preservation, we have seen this evolve into a highly complex system of norms, laws, and policies, all of which are shaped by a web of state and nonstate actors, and for-profit and not-for-profit institutions.[16] Yet within this network of networks, the state appears to be an enduringly powerful actor. Given that international organizations such as UNESCO remain "flimsy," as Thomas Weiss puts it, often lacking the resources to enact their worldview, the state remains a key force exerting its will upon the cultural past.[17] It is important to recognize that the ongoing incorporation of cultural-sector international cooperation into other streams of humanitarian and developmental aid means questions surrounding neo-imperialism and dependency structures become ever more pertinent to the preservation sector. The analytical frames of venues, cooperation, and borders have been offered here as part of an approach intended to open up such questions and lines of enquiry previously ignored by scholars in a variety of fields, concerning the layered and fascinating entanglements between the past and the enterprise of preserving its material culture, and our unfolding histories of globalization and international affairs.

Biography
Tim Winter is president of the Association of Critical Heritage Studies and research professor in Cultural Heritage at Deakin University, Melbourne. He has published widely on heritage, development, urban conservation, tourism, and heritage diplo-

macy. He has been a visiting scholar at the University of Cambridge, Getty Conservation Institute, and Asia Research Institute, Singapore. Recent books include *The Routledge Handbook of Heritage in Asia* and *Shanghai Expo: An International Forum on the Future of Cities.*

Notes

This work was supported by the Australia Research Council Discovery Scheme under Grant DP140102991—The Crisis in International Heritage Conservation in an Age of Shifting Global Power.

[1] Notable examples here include J. Jokilehto, *History of Architectural Conservation* (Oxford: Butterworth-Heinemann, 1999); M. Glendinning, *The Conservation Movement: A History of Architectural Preservation, Antiquity to Modernity* (London: Routledge, 2013); Astrid Swenson and Peter Mandler, eds., *From Plunder to Preservation: Britain and the Heritage of Empire, 1800–1950,* Proceedings of the British Academy 187 (Oxford: Oxford University Press, 2013); J. P. Singh, *United Nations Educational, Scientific, and Cultural Organization (UNESCO): Creating Norms for a Complex World* (New York: Routledge, 2011).

[2] Tim Winter "Heritage Diplomacy," in *International Journal of Heritage Studies* 21, no. 10 (2015): 917–1015.

[3] UNESCO (United Nations Educational, Scientific, and Cultural Organization); ICOM (International Council of Monuments); ICCROM (International Centre for the Study of the Preservation and Restoration of Cultural Property); and ICOMOS (International Council on Monuments and Sites).

[4] Astrid Swenson, *The Rise of Heritage: Preserving the Past in France, Germany, and England, 1789–1914* (Cambridge: Cambridge University Press, 2013) and D. M. Reid, *Whose Pharaohs? Archaeology, Museums, and Egyptian National Identity from Napoleon to World War I* (Berkeley: University of California Press, 2002).

[5] L. Allias, "The Design of the Nubian Desert: Monuments, Mobility, and the Space of Global Culture," in *Governing by Design: Architecture, Economy, and Politics in the Twentieth Century,* ed., Aggregate Group, 179–215 (Pittsburgh: University of Pittsburgh Press, 2012)..

[6] UNESCO, *Nubia: A Triumph of International Solidarity* (Paris: UNESCO, 1982).

[7] For detailed account of this process see T. Winter, *Post-Conflict Heritage, Postcolonial Tourism: Culture, Politics, and Development at Angkor* (London: Routledge, 2007).

[8] GDP (Gross Domestic Product).

[9] For further details see, Bruno Latour, *Reassembling the Social: An Introduction to Actor-Network Theory* (Oxford: Oxford University Press, 2007), and for examples of this theory for the preservation and heritage fields see, S. Macdonald, "Reassembling Nuremberg, Reassembling Culture," *Journal of Cultural Economy* 2, no. 1 (2009): 117–34, and R. Harrison, *Heritage: Critical Approaches* (London: Routledge, 2013).

[10] See M. Beyen, "Art and Architectural History as Substitutes for Preservation: German Heritage Policy in Belgium during and after the First World War," 32–43, and W. Cortjaens, "'The German Way of Making Better Cities': German Reconstruction Plans for Belgium during the First World War," 44–58, both in *Living with History, 1914–1964: Rebuilding Europe after the First and Second World Wars and the Role of Heritage Preservation,* eds. N. Bullock and L. Verpoest (Leuven: Leuven University Press, 2011).

[11] M. Singh, "PM's Speech at the Banquet Hosted by President of Myanmar," May 28, 2012, http://pmindia.nic.in/speech-details.php?nodeid=1178.

[12] Quoted from N. Dholabhai and A. Mohan, "China Niggle in Myanmar Ties," *The Telegraph* (Calcutta, India), July 22, 2010, www.telegraphindia.com/1100722/jsp /frontpage/story_12712529.jsp.

[13] T. Winter, "Heritage Conservation Futures in an Age of Shifting Global Power," *Journal of Social Archaeology* 14, no. 3 (2014): 319–39.

[14] Christine Sylvester, *Art/Museums: International Relations Where We Least Expect It* (Boulder, Colo.: Paradigm Publishers, 2009).

[15] T. Winter, "Beyond Eurocentrism? Heritage Conservation and the Politics of Difference," *International Journal of Heritage Studies* 20, no. 2 (2014): 123–37.

[16] For further details, see F. Francioni and J. Gordley, eds, *Enforcing International Cultural Heritage Law* (Oxford: Oxford University Press, 2013), and R. Harrison, *Heritage: Critical Approaches* (London: Routledge, 2013).

[17] T. G. Weiss, *Global Governance: Why? What? Whither?* (Cambridge, U.K.: Polity, 2013), 143.

1. Penn Museum expedition house, Mit Rahina, Egypt, 1955. Courtesy of Penn Museum.

William Carruthers

Multilateral Possibilities
Decolonization, Preservation, and the Case of Egypt

How did the rapid growth of multilateralism and international collaboration after World War II (re-)constitute preservation practices in decolonizing countries? In order to overcome structural imbalances in international organizations like UNESCO, responses to this question have often argued that postwar preservation work reflected a neocolonialist frame.[1] I do not dispute the inequalities that UNESCO and related institutions embody, nor do I dispute the necessity of overcoming them. But in this article, I am more interested in starting to understand the actions behind the production of such inequalities. Rather than taking these inequalities as natural, this understanding can provide an account of the forms of power that produced such imbalances and usefully highlight their historical contingency. As Tim Winter notes, "to label the founding of the new post-war intergovernmental landscape as merely Eurocentric or neo-imperialist would miss the important political spaces it would open up."[2] In this article, I use Winter's observation to think through the matter of preservation work in postwar Egypt, illustrating the growth of a multilateral discourse superficially benefiting Euro-Americans concerned with the excavation and preservation of ancient antiquities and architecture. Conversely, I then demonstrate how that discourse helped to materialize novel forms of Egyptian power.

Egypt provides an excellent case study. A well-known literature frames work related to ancient Egyptian remains squarely in terms of colonial-era contestation.[3] Yet (how) did the history of contestation around such artifacts and architecture enable new modes of political power to become manifest there? The one substantive work dealing with this question concludes in the early 1940s, despite its author's recognition that this temporal boundary is arbitrary.[4] What happened after 1945 as Britain's presence in Egypt weakened, the country's monarch, Faruq, became increasingly unpopular, and various Egyptian and regional movements promoted political change?[5] Before the war, many foreigners had become concerned about their ability to continue working with ancient Egyptian remains in the country. But what happened after 1945, as events gathered pace and, ultimately, Nasser became figurehead of a revolutionary nation-state? In what follows, I detail Egyptian responses to the forms of multilateralism that emerged around this time in relation to excavation and preservation work on

Future Anterior
Volume XIII, Number 1
Summer 2016

the country's ancient material culture. By doing so, I illustrate how these responses fused ancient remains with the alphabet soup of multilateralism in order to instantiate those remains as constitutive of political revolution.

Multilateralism and Ancient Egyptian Material Culture: Beginnings

First, though, I discuss the prehistory of these responses in order to illustrate the conditions that helped to form them. After 1945, the material culture of ancient Egypt had become embedded within the growing multilateral arena. To adopt multilateralism meant taking heed of a change in the way order in the world was represented; practitioners concerned with excavating and preserving Egypt's ancient past were as likely to value this representation as others. Yet paying attention to multilateralism also meant reinforcing the unbalanced sort of governance that multilateral institutions tended to generate.

In August 1947, less than two years after the Charter of the United Nations came into being, an international group of Egyptologists gathered at the University of Copenhagen to discuss the future of a discipline many of whose members (philologists, archaeologists, and architects with an interest in ancient Egyptian material culture) had been riven apart by the Second World War.[6] Reflecting residual tension relating to the conflict, Germans had not been invited, but representatives came to the meeting from Belgium, Britain, Czechoslovakia, Denmark, Egypt, France, Holland, Poland, Sweden, Switzerland, and the United States. Their gathering resulted in the foundation of an International Association of Egyptologists (IAE). The IAE (as this initial gathering suggests) was a veritable United Nations of the Egyptological world. Indeed, the organization promised that Germans could gain their membership if and when Germany (at that point still one country) became accredited as a member of the fledgling UNESCO.[7] Yet such conditionality also suggests that a primary purpose of the IAE was conducting "boundary work": asking questions about (and also regulating) not only who could be an Egyptologist but also what sort of work they could conduct.[8]

Much of the boundary work that occurred at Copenhagen seems innocuous. During the meeting, attendees discussed whether a new ancient Egyptian dictionary project should be started and based in Copenhagen. They also asked whether Egyptologists should publish articles outside of the discipline's established journals. Beyond such discussions, though, attendees also formed a series of regulatory committees to advance the multilateral regulation of Egyptological practice, creating familiar issues related to such governance. For instance, the IAE's steering committee was to be formed

of eleven members from eleven different countries. Predict-
ably, one representative was to be from the United States and
another from the Soviet Union. Yet pointing to the way in which
multilateral governance also helped to marginalize countries
emerging from colonialism, only one representative was to be
Egyptian: Sami Gabra, a (British- and French-trained) archaeologist from Fu'ad (now Cairo) University.[9] Given a long tradition
of such marginalization during Egyptology's colonial development, it is difficult not to interpret this act as much other than a
use of multilateral rhetoric to perpetuate a status quo privileging foreign access to ancient Egyptian material.[10] At the time,
at least one Egyptian Egyptologist stated that "through . . . the
co-operation of scholars of all nations, Egyptology will undoubtedly prosper."[11] But the multilateral and internationalist
rhetoric that they used also acted against their influence.

The IAE, as Donald Reid has noted, was "still-born."[12] But
institutional failure does not mean that the sort of boundary
work the IAE enacted did not live on elsewhere. Even after
the Egyptian Free Officers' coup of 1952, examples exist of
international collaboration around ancient Egyptian remains
promoting the continued primacy of European work relating
to them. The coup heralded not only the start of Nasser's rise
to power but also the installation of the first Egyptian director
of the country's Antiquities Service, now renamed the Department of Antiquities. Mustafa Amer was a geographer and pre-
historian who believed in scientific internationalism; many of
the Egyptian staff he managed held similar ideals.[13] Particular
foreign institutions interested in excavating in Egypt now took
clear advantage of this situation, even as they also asserted
the value of the work that they conducted in terms of the scientific recovery and preservation of the country's past.

For instance, in 1953, Britain's Egypt Exploration Society
(EES) gained a concession to dig at the site of Saqqara "on
behalf of, and in collaboration with, the Department of Antiquities."[14] This internationalist language, however, was pure
rhetoric: committee minutes reveal that the work provided an
excuse to continue the earlier work of the British organization's
new Field Director, the archaeologist Walter Bryan Emery, who
had excavated monumental tombs at the site while working
for the Antiquities Service in the interwar period. Minutes
also reveal that the EES's committee saw the discovery and
preservation of such tombs as providing a potential means of
obtaining ancient Egyptian artifacts, presumably to distribute
to supporters.[15] There is little doubt that Emery believed in the
scientific importance of the work that he carried out. Yet there
is also little doubt that he (and the institution that backed him)
used the language of international collaboration to enable
more cynical motives, too.

2. Penn Museum excavations at Mit Rahina, Egypt, 1955. Courtesy of Penn Museum.

Nor was this practice limited to European institutions. During 1955 and 1956, the then-University Museum of the University of Pennsylvania (UM; now the University of Pennsylvania Museum of Archaeology and Anthropology) conducted a collaborative excavation with the Department of Antiquities at the site of Mit Rahina (ancient Memphis), just south of Cairo.[16] To a large degree, collaboration in this case was again formulated to fit the foreign institution's plans. Despite Egyptians (including Amer) making the initial moves, the excavation (novel in purpose) was formulated as the sort of technical assistance exercise promoted under the rubric of Truman's Point Four program: a rubric that used such modernization work to embed American values in countries considered useful Cold War allies. In this instance, the UM (acting without the backing of the U.S. government) offered to transfer archaeological skills at the same time as excavating a site that most of the Department of Antiquities was keen to return to agricultural use; the Free Officers had instigated a policy of limited land reform and redistribution, and Mit Rahina was of potential agricultural value.[17] The process of working out where at Mit Rahina excavation might continue — and which parts of the site should be preserved — would (or so its Board of Managers hoped) enable the American institution to embed itself in Egypt, giving it (like the EES) the prolonged opportunity to transport excavated artifacts back to Philadelphia. Rudolf Anthes, the German-born Egyptologist who the UM placed in charge of the excavation, believed in the progressive nature of the work that his field team would carry out. But, once again, collaboration also had ulterior motives.

3. Penn Museum excavations at Mit Rahina, Egypt, 1955. Courtesy of Penn Museum.

My concern in the remainder of this essay, however, is not in the details of such collaborative excavations per se. Instead, what interests me is the way that such international collaboration around material culture—and the growth of multilateralism in relation to the preservation of Egypt's past more generally—started to enable Egyptian authorities to channel their own political wishes. Both the programmatic technical collaboration advanced by the UM and also the much more lackadaisical collaboration of the EES failed, and failed due to the policies of the Egyptian government. To understand this process, I turn to another collaborative project involving the Department of Antiquities.

Preserving Ancient Nubia, Multilaterally

In late 1955, the Department of Antiquities published a volume entitled *Report on the Monuments of Nubia Likely to Be Submerged by Sudd-el-ʿĀli Water.* The *Report* appeared as plans gathered pace for the construction of the new Aswan High Dam (the *Sudd-el-ʿĀli*), which was rapidly becoming the centerpiece of Egypt's revolution.[18] Within the publication's pages, a committee of upper-level Department members attempted to regulate how the ancient monuments of Egyptian Nubia could be preserved and the sort of knowledge that could be gleaned from them recorded before the reservoir (now Lake Nasser) that would form behind the dam submerged them forever. The *Report* (written in Arabic, English, and French) constituted the

ancient past as part of the contemporary process of revolutionary environmental transformation in Nubia. Moreover, it formalized this process of transformation as multilateral, attempting
to make Nubia's ancient material culture a "boundary object"
around which various international interests could gather and
subverting the strategy that foreign institutions had previously
used.[19] At the publication's beginning, a reproduction of a letter from the Egyptologist Salim Hassan, leader of the departmental committee, assured Kamal al-Din Hussein, Egypt's
Minister of Education, "that Egypt . . . is capable of carrying out
this project." Yet Hassan also noted "the hearty welcome of the
Egyptian archaeologists to the assistance of some of their foreign colleagues," stating "that if UNESCO has any intention of
presenting any pecuniary, material or scientific aid to Egypt . . .
we have to thank it deeply."[20]

Several years later, in 1960, UNESCO launched an appeal on behalf of the Egyptian and Sudanese governments for
what would become its International Campaign to Save the
Monuments of Nubia.[21] A recent critical article (as does much
official literature) seems to suggest that this event took place
almost *sui generis* and was, to a significant extent, the result
of UNESCO's agency.[22] Yet the 1955 *Report* begs us to rethink
this interpretation: the publication makes it clear that plans for
the Nubian campaign (and related attempts to make UNESCO
become involved with it) were afoot long before 1960. Why,
then, do these plans now seem almost forgotten? I argue that
the transfer of agency to the multilateral auspices of UNESCO
acted as a means (now lodged in the historiography) to conceal
the way in which the Egyptian government had realized that it
could start to use foreign interactions with ancient material culture in order to assert and represent its own political wishes.
Constituting the Nubian campaign as a boundary object also
meant constituting a novel set of power relations.

The EES and the UM may have drawn on multilateralism
and the rhetoric of collaboration to work in Egypt, but now the
Egyptian government used this rhetoric in an attempt not only
to regulate the practices of such institutions as they carried out
their work but also to manage the country's wider political interests. The *Report* was one step in this process. Another step
(also in 1955) involved moving beyond the publication's internationalist rhetoric and mobilizing the resources of UNESCO
in order to constitute the institutional framework within which
this collaboration could be managed. That year, the Centre
d'Étude et de Documentation sur l'Ancienne Égypte (or CEDAE)
was established. CEDAE aimed to prepare for the forthcoming
Nubian work by documenting antiquities, archaeological
sites, and ancient monuments across the region and the wider
country, and was formed under the terms of the UN's Expanded

Program of Technical Assistance. The agency resulted, then, from an official request made by Egypt's Ministry of Education to UNESCO. And in a government memo establishing CEDAE's formal basis within Egypt, Kamal al-Din Hussein emphasized the work that such a multilateral strategy could do for the country's revolutionary future.

Writing in April 1955, the minister stated that CEDAE could be "a source for equipping them [Egyptians] with the history of human civilization," confirming that Egypt constituted an example of a "universal civilization" ("ḥaḍāra ʿālamiyya") and thereby using the sort of language promoted under UNESCO's auspices.[23] But at the same time as using this language, Hussein also drew on contemporary rhetoric dealing with the reform of the Egyptian peasantry in order to stress that the institution could be "a means of educating sons of the country."[24] Furthermore, Hussein specified that a major rationale for CEDAE's establishment centered on concerns that "many antiquities were exported outside Egypt without registration."[25] CEDAE had a revolutionary ordering mission, which the Arabic version of the agency's name made clear: the Markaz Tasjil al-Athar al-Misriyya was the Centre for Registering (*tasjīl*) Egyptian Antiquities. Placing work relating to Egyptian antiquities within the multilateral realm could help to constitute Egyptian property and population, ancient and modern, whether in Nubia or more widely.

Of course, this strategy came with conditions. Like other collaborative work, the foundation of CEDAE constituted expertise relating to Egypt's (now universal) civilization as linked to an institutional world outside the country. The agreement establishing the Centre stated that CEDAE was founded "in light of recommendations in the report by the head of the UNESCO mission of experts" that had studied the initial Egyptian proposal. That mission head was the Egyptologist Christiane Desroches Noblecourt of the Louvre, and her recommendations included not only working practices, but also matters relating to "employees and an appropriate budget."[26] Yet even as Noblecourt headed CEDAE, this situation created opportunities for Egypt: the directives of the UN Program allowed that Egyptian officials become involved with carrying out work at the agency, too.

More than other collaborative work taking place in the country, CEDAE therefore gave Egyptians a hand as their government pushed for foreign institutions to undertake excavation and preservation work in Nubia: the agency constituted Egypt's past as a universal civilization, but to do so it required accession to local demands as a matter of (almost moral) course.[27] Retiring from the leadership of the Department of Antiquities, Amer became CEDAE's Egyptian director.[28] Years later, Noblecourt reminisced that her work with CEDAE meant that "je fis la connaissance du professeur Mustafa Amer, dont la courtoisie et l'intelligence me sédusirent." She also complimented Amer for his work in the Department of Antiquities, which she said that he had "insuffler un sang neuf [infused with a fresh blood], inspire par les expériences les plus modernes."[29] Noblecourt of course represented her dealings with Amer in this way: she wanted to suggest that their cooperation had been driven by a shared, internationalist belief in progress (which, to an extent, was true). Yet by acknowledging Amer's influence, her statement also confirms the leverage that Egyptian officials enjoyed as their work became embroiled within multilateral discourse. As the Department of Antiquities continued to push for international collaboration in Nubia, these conditions meant that it would be difficult to ignore its requests. To do otherwise would be to undermine the apparently benign cultural cooperation that such conditions promoted.

Making Multilateralism Stick

Unfortunately for them, foreign institutions working in Egypt often ignored these conditions. The UM's work at Mit Rahina provides a case in point. During the excavation's second season in 1956, Anthes wrote to the institution's director, Froelich Rainey, and informed him of Amer's forthcoming move to CEDAE. He noted that "although I should no means recommend striking after a close connection . . . it seems to be wise to be present at work when the Center fully develops."[30] In Egypt, Anthes could see the course that events relating to antiquities were taking. But back in Philadelphia, no one listened to his advice, and the result was a clash with an emboldened Department of Antiquities. Multilateralism mattered.

A distinct lack of success at Mit Rahina constituted the grounds for this clash. Excavating the site meant dealing with a confusing assortment of waterlogged architectural remains, and the planned transfer of archaeological skills there had failed, sunk in the site's murky depths. Moreover, excavating this complex ancient settlement (a difficult process that was itself out of the ordinary in Egypt) did not yield the sort of ancient artifacts that the UM wanted to acquire. Acting unilaterally, the institution—and in particular its Board—therefore decided to end the collaborative excavations at the site: at first postponing a planned third season of work (using the 1956 Suez conflict and its aftermath as an excuse) but then cancelling it altogether.[31] The Board agreed that the funds set aside for the work could be used to excavate elsewhere in the country "at some future date."[32] But this outcome—particularly in terms of the UM's desire to choose the location of such an excavation—did not arise, because the Department of Antiquities now decided to call the shots. If the UM chose to adopt multilateral rhetoric, the Department would force the institution to stick to that rhetoric or face the consequences. And in a climate of Cold War paranoia and revolutionary posturing, those consequences caused no small amount of concern.

After Suez, a Polish archaeological mission had started excavating the mound of Tell Atrib, located just outside the Nile Delta city of Benha. While not excavating in the Department's preferred location of Nubia, these representatives of the Warsaw Pact still looked magnanimous as they dug. In September 1957, the (government-produced) *Egypt Travel Magazine,* distributed worldwide, made clear that excavations at the site (a series of settlement layers in the Nile's cultivation) fit well with the sort of work that Egypt promoted through an agency like CEDAE, because the excavations overcame the issue that "on cultivated lands the mounds are a nuisance and are steadily cut into. Hunters for antiques do further damage." Now these mounds and the antiquities within them were registered and regulated, allowing the magazine to claim that apart from Tell Atrib "no continuously inhabited town site from ancient Egypt has ever been properly excavated," despite the site's distinct similarity to Mit Rahina.[33] This apparent Polish success caused deep disquiet. For example, the *Newsletter* of the American Research Center in Egypt noted that the Polish work had come about "as part of the cultural exchange between Egypt and Communist countries" and that "the [Egyptian] government is extending to them many courtesies and privileges." Worse still, these courtesies included artifacts: "at the end of last year's excavation at Benha, the Polish Expedition was permitted to take back to Poland a share of the finds it has made."[34] Reacting to this situation, Helen Wall, a member of the UM's Mit Rahina team, told Anthes that if Western countries did not "fill that cultural vacuum," then "the Egyptians will be forced to take people from the Russian zone."[35]

The Department of Antiquities exploited this paranoia. Even before Rainey had written to the department to cancel the Mit Rahina work, he reported that "he had received a letter from the Egyptian Government cancelling the Museum's contract to work at Memphis. They have requested us to work at Nubia [*sic*]."[36] Echoing the Department's earlier *Report,* this letter, sent in October 1957, enclosed a list of Nubian sites, making clear that the UM could relocate its work only to these locations. The UM could either excavate in Nubia or forget about excavating in Egypt at all, leaving the country (and the future of its revolution) to archaeologists like the Poles.[37] Meanwhile, other institutions also received the Department's letter; the EES's concerned committee concluded that "there was . . . no promising site among those listed."[38] The Department appeared to have engineered a *fait accompli*. Representing multilateral collaboration around ancient Egyptian material culture as taking the form of a benign boundary object allowed the Department to direct where excavation would occur and perhaps even how. As Egypt asserted revolution, potential spaces of excavation—and the sorts of material held within them—played a meaningful role.

Conclusion

In postwar Egypt, making use of multilateral discourse relating to the excavation and preservation of ancient material culture allowed the country to assert its revolutionary wishes using (the promise of) interactions with the monuments and antiquities that that material culture comprised. The events detailed above only represent the start of this story. Despite the ultimatum that the Department of Antiquities presented to foreign institutions in 1957, the wholesale undertaking of archaeological work in Nubia remained uncertain and only became a reality when UNESCO advanced its involvement beyond CEDAE to back a wider Nubian campaign. Egypt had to push the practice of multilateralism further than it perhaps wanted to. I do not have space to detail that process here, but the discussion above suggests that multilateralism ultimately made for uncomfortable archaeological bedfellows in Nubia, despite the internationalist rhetoric now attached to the eventual campaign there.

This situation prompts two thoughts. First, we need to reexamine what we think we know about the Nubian campaign. Little critical analysis has been directed toward the Nubian work, and the campaign is generally interpreted as a rare (preservationist) monument to internationalism in an otherwise heated political context. To what extent, then, was the utopia of the Nubian campaign a reality if, prior to its commencement, Egypt used multilateralism as a boundary object to assert itself in the face of the cynical use of such rhetoric by others? Only in-depth study will tell. Second, we also need to pry open the foundation myth attached to the Nubian work: that impetus for the creation of the 1972 World Heritage Convention to a great extent derived from the carrying out of the campaign there.[39] Given events outlined above, (how) did countries reach agreement about the Convention at the same time as they played political games with each other? To what extent did World Heritage constitute a further boundary object to neutralize political battles around preservation and related fields? Only a nuanced understanding of the Nubian campaign will enable us to answer these questions.

Biography
William Carruthers is a Gerda Henkel Stiftung postdoctoral Research Scholar and also visiting guest scholar at the German Historical Institute London. He holds a PhD (2014) in history and philosophy of science from the University of Cambridge, and is the editor of *Histories of Egyptology: Interdisciplinary Measures* (2014). He can be contacted at: carruthers@ghil.ac.uk.

Notes
This paper is based on PhD research undertaken in the Department of History and Philosophy of Science at the University of Cambridge, and supported by grants from the UK Arts and Humanities Research Council, Darwin College (University of Cambridge), the German Academic Exchange Service, the H. M. Chadwick Fund (University of Cambridge), and the Royal Historical Society. Thanks to Walter Armbrust, Eleanor Robson, Jim Secord, Simon Schaffer, and Tim Winter for their help.
[1] See e.g. Susan Wright, "The Politicization of 'Culture,'" *Anthropology Today* 14 (1998): 7–15.
[2] Tim Winter, "Heritage Diplomacy," *International Journal of Heritage Studies* 21 (2015): 1002. For these political spaces as they developed in relation to UNESCO, see Lynn Meskell, "UNESCO's World Heritage Convention at 40: Challenging the Economic and Political Order of International Heritage Conservation," *Current Anthropology* 54 (2013): 483–94.
[3] Elliott Colla, *Conflicted Antiquities: Egyptology, Egyptomania, Egyptian Modernity* (Durham, N.C.: Duke University Press, 2007); Donald Malcolm Reid, *Whose Pharaohs? Archaeology, Museums, and Egyptian National Identity from Napoleon to World War I* (Berkeley: University of California Press, 2002).
[4] Colla, *Conflicted Antiquities*, 275–76. Cf. Donald Malcolm Reid, *Contesting Antiquity in Egypt: Archaeologies, Museums and the Struggle for Identities from World War I to Nasser* (Cairo and New York: The American University in Cairo Press, 2015), which only became available after this article was accepted for publication.
[5] For the best overview of this political process, see Joel Gordon, *Nasser's Blessed Movement: Egypt's Free Officers and the July Revolution* (New York: Oxford University Press, 1992).
[6] Stephen Quirke, *Hidden Hands: Egyptian Workforces in Petrie Excavation Archives, 1880–1924* (London: Duckworth, 2010), 4, discusses the complexity of defining Egyptology.
[7] Herbert Ricke to Rudolf Anthes, Uvo Hölscher, and Alexander Scharff, August 30, 1947, file 001, Rudolf Anthes Teilnachlass, Archiv der Staatlichen Museen zu Berlin.
[8] For boundary work, see Thomas F. Gieryn, "Boundary-Work and the Demarcation of Science from Non-Science: Strains and Interests in Professional Ideologies of Scientists," *American Sociological Review* 48 (1983): 781–95.
[9] *Supra* note 7.
[10] Reid, *Whose Pharaohs?*, explores this marginalization in detail.
[11] Mustafa el-Amir, "The Birth and Growth of Egyptology," *The Bulletin Issued by the Egyptian Education Bureau* 40 (1949): 21. El-Amir was an Egyptologist specialized in Demotic texts.
[12] Donald Malcolm Reid, "Nationalizing the Pharaonic Past: Egyptology, Imperialism, and Egyptian Nationalism, 1922–1952," in *Rethinking Nationalism in the Arab Middle East,* ed. Israel Gershoni and James Jankowski (New York: Columbia University Press, 1997), 147.
[13] For Amer, see Omnia El Shakry, *The Great Social Laboratory: Subjects of Knowledge in Colonial and Postcolonial Egypt* (Stanford, Calif.: Stanford University Press, 2007), 68.
[14] Walter Bryan Emery, *Excavations at Sakkara: Great Tombs of the First Dynasty II* (London: Egypt Exploration Society and Oxford University Press, 1954), vii.
[15] Minutes of the Egypt Exploration Society Executive Committee, May 19, 1954, Egypt Exploration Society Committee Minutes volume for 1942–1955, Egypt Exploration Society Lucy Gura Archive, London.
[16] I explore the excavation in more detail in William Carruthers, "Grounding Ideologies: Archaeology, Decolonization, and the Cold War in Egypt," in *Decolonization and the Cold War: Negotiating Independence,* ed. Leslie James and Elisabeth Leake, 167–82 (London: Bloomsbury Academic, 2015).
[17] For land reform and Point Four in Egypt, see Jon B. Alterman, *Egypt and American Foreign Assistance, 1952–1956* (Basingstoke, U.K.: Palgrave, 2002).
[18] Maslihat al-Athar [Department of Antiquities], *Report on the Monuments of Nubia Likely to Be Submerged by Sudd-el-ʿĀli Water* (Cairo: Government Press, 1955); for the lengthy genesis of the High Dam, see Ahmad Shokr, "Hydropolitics, Economy, and the Aswan High Dam in Mid-Century Egypt," *The Arab Studies Journal* 17 (2009): 9–31.

[19] For boundary objects, see e.g. Étienne Wenger, *Communities of Practice: Learning, Meaning, and Identity* (Cambridge: Cambridge University Press, 1998).

[20] Maslihat al-Athar, *Report,* vii–viii.

[21] The construction of the Aswan High Dam would lead to the flooding of Sudanese Nubia, too.

[22] Paul Betts, "The Warden of World Heritage: UNESCO and the Rescue of the Nubian Monuments," *Past and Present,* supplement 10 (2015): 100–25.

[23] Memo written by Kamal al-Din Hussein, April 25, 1955, file 0081–003715, Egyptian National Archives, Cairo.

[24] Ibid. The Nasserist regime used the Egyptian non-elite signifier of "sons of the country" (*awlād al-balad*; sing. *ibn al-balad*) to stress a positive identity for the Egyptian peasantry. For the history of this term, see Sawsan el-Messiri, *Ibn al-Balad: A Concept of Egyptian Identity* (Leiden, The Netherlands.: E. J. Brill, 1978).

[25] *Supra* note 23.

[26] Ibid.

[27] For the UN's Expanded Program of Technical Assistance as it took place in Egypt at this time, see Cornelis Arthur Pompe, "The United Nations in Egypt: A Survey of its Organisations—Their Background Functions and Immunities," *Revue égyptienne de droit international* 13 (1957): 49–62.

[28] Morris L. Bierbrier, *Who Was Who in Egyptology,* 4th ed. (London: Egypt Exploration Society, 2012), 17–18.

[29] Christiane Desroches Noblecourt, *La grande Nubiade, ou, le parcours d'une égyptologue* (Paris: Stock/Pernoud, 1992), 125. Translations: "I met Professor Mustafa Amer, whose courtesy and intelligence charmed me" and "infused with a fresh blood, inspired by the most modern experiences."

[30] Rudolf Anthes to Froelich Rainey, April 9, 1956, Mit Rahina records, box 38, folder 7, archives of the University of Pennsylvania Museum of Archaeology and Anthropology, Philadelphia (UMA).

[31] For further details see note 16.

[32] Froelich Rainey to Percy Madeira, October 15, 1957, Egypt records, box 46, folder 1, UMA.

[33] Rowland Ellis [oddly, an American writer], "Poland Digs in Egypt," *Egypt Travel Magazine,* September 1957, 12–16.

[34] Edward Wente, "Letter [untitled]," *American Research Center in Egypt, Incorporated: Newsletter* 26 (1957): 4.

[35] Helen Wall to Rudolf Anthes, May 4, 1957, Mit Rahina records, box 38, folder 9, UMA.

[36] Minutes of the University Museum Board of Managers, December 10, 1957, Minutes of the University Museum Board of Managers volume for 1953–1959, UMA.

[37] Moharram Kamal to Froelich Rainey, October 31, 1957, Egypt records, box 46, folder 1, UMA.

[38] Minutes of the Egypt Exploration Society Executive Committee, March 27, 1958, Egypt Exploration Society Committee Minutes volume for 1956–1963, Egypt Exploration Society Lucy Gura Archive, London.

[39] See e.g. Torgny Säve-Söderbergh, *Temples and Tombs of Ancient Nubia: The International Rescue Campaign at Abu Simbel, Philae, and Other Sites* (London and Paris: Thames and Hudson and UNESCO, 1987). Work starting to prise apart (certain) elements of the Nubian campaign has come to my attention since this article was accepted for publication: Lucia Allais, "The Design of the Nubian Desert: Monuments, Mobility, and the Space of Global Culture," in *Governing by Design: Architecture, Economy, and Politics in the Twentieth Century,* ed. Aggregate (Architectural History Collaborative), 179–215 (Pittsburgh: University of Pittsburgh Press, 2012); Lucia Allais, "Integrities: The Salvage of Abu Simbel," *Grey Room* 50 (2013): 6–45.

19 Historic Scotland, "New 3D Sydney Opera House Scanning Now Underway," press release, April 18, 2013.

20 "New 3D Sydney Opera House Unveiled for its 40th Anniversary," press release, November 14, 2013.

21 "Japan Selected as Final International Site for Scottish Ten," press release, August 11, 2014; "Japan Trip Journal," Scottish Ten, http://www.scottishten.org/index/news/nagasakiblog.htm.

22 Ibid.

23 Ibid.

24 UNESCO, "Rani-ki-Vav (the Queen's Stepwell) at Patan, Gujarat," *UNESCO.org*, http://whc.unesco.org/en/list/922; "Sites of Japan's Meiji Industrial Revolution: Iron and Steel, Shipbuilding and Coal Mining," *UNESCO.org*, http://whc.unesco.org/en/list/1484.

25 Historic Scotland, *Annual Report & Accounts 2012–2013* (Edinburgh: Historic Scotland, 2013), 9.

26 Historic Scotland, "Historic Scotland Launch."; "First Images of Laser Scan Chinese Tombs," news release, November 10, 2012; "Sydney Opera House to be."; "New 3D Sydney"; "Unveiled for its 40th"; "Japan Selected as Final"; Parth Shastri, "Ranki vav Posed Technical Challenge: Scottish Experts," *Times of India,* November 7, 2011, Factiva Database.

27 "Plans to Celebrate Conservationist," *Herald* (Glasgow), April 8, 2013, 5; David Ross, "Childhood Home of John Muir Digitally Scanned," *Herald* (Glasgow), September 19, 2013, 12.

28 Historic Scotland, "Scottish Ten—What's Next?" *ScottishTen.org,* http://www.scottishten.org/index/about.htm.

29 Natarajan, "Digital Public Diplomacy and a Strategic Narrative for India," 91–106.

1. The seventeenth-century Fort Nieuw Victoria, here photographed in 1925, was once a key bastion of the VOC in the Indonesian archipelago and an example of the kind of overseas monuments that would capture van Overvoorde's interest centuries later. Courtesy of Leiden University Library (image code 12963).

Lauren Yapp

Define *Mutual*
Heritage Diplomacy in the
Postcolonial Netherlands

In 1910, Jacob Cornelis van Overvoorde—archivist, curator, and amateur archaeologist—was called upon by the government of the Netherlands to compile an inventory of Dutch monuments of history and art. The ministers, however, got perhaps more than they had bargained for in delegating this task to an individual described even by friends as "anything but a smooth and easy man . . . [with a] fidelity to the principle adopted . . . perseverance . . . dutiful industriousness, that never-ending work, and tenacity which was even in the face of death unbreakable."[1] Indeed, van Overvoorde interpreted his assignment to include not merely the stately homes or aging churches that fell within the borders of the Low Countries but also to encompass the entire breadth of tangible traces left behind by prior generations of Dutch merchants and settlers in the forms of fortifications, warehouses, city blocks, churches, and the like scattered across three continents.

Lamenting the lack of an overseas preservation strategy on the part of the Hague for what he felt to be these self-evidently "Dutch" monuments abroad, van Overvoorde soon took it upon himself to set off on a round-the-world tour to document these far-flung vestiges of the VOC (the Dutch East India Company), the WIC (the Dutch West India Company), and other colonial ventures. An ambitious project even by today's standards—to complete his inventory, van Overvoorde planned to travel first to South Africa, India, and Sri Lanka, where a formerly robust Dutch presence had long been supplanted by subsequent waves of foreign imperialism, before then moving on to Indonesia, Suriname, and several islands in the Lesser Antilles, which remained, at that time at least, firmly part of the Dutch empire. Unfortunately for the intrepid van Overvoorde (and for curious contemporary scholars), it all turned out to be a bit of a flop: forced by deteriorating health to abandon his journey at the halfway mark and eventually publishing only a small fraction of the findings from the truncated trip, his work ultimately fell far short of the global ambit of his original intentions.[2]

Why revisit here, if only briefly, a failed project that petered out over a century ago? First, van Overvoorde's travels foreshadow the aspirations, object, and scope of the contemporary phenomenon that concerns this article—that is, the Mutual (sometimes also termed "Shared" or "Common") Cultural Heritage Programme promoted by the Dutch government as a

Future Anterior
Volume XIII, Number 1
Summer 2016

keystone of their international cultural policy and as a channel through which to improve relations with former colonies and other states with which the Netherlands has had significant interaction in the past. Second, his journey underscores a core theme that will be explored here, one that may seem implied when speaking of heritage but in fact is often overlooked in the rather presentist field of "heritage studies"—that is, history, or rather historical specificity, matters. Particular colonial experiences in the past generate, or perpetuate, particular strategies and methods of heritage diplomacy in the present. And while heritage diplomacy in practice appears to be, and indeed often is, concerned primarily with the pursuit of immediate economic or political aims in an international arena, its execution also can speak on a more profound level to how nations struggle internally to understand their own pasts and the ways in which that specific historical experience continues to condition attitudes and actions.

The Mutual Cultural Heritage Programme
While van Overvoorde's unsuccessful travels may have set an early precedent, to trace the more immediate origins of the Mutual Cultural Heritage Programme (sometimes here referred to as MCH) we need to jump forward in time, past wars, revolutions, and coups that stripped the Netherlands of virtually all its colonies (save for a few tiny islands). While the Dutch nation and empire had long been overshadowed by its French and British parallels, by the 1980s the Netherlands truly had to come to terms with the reality that its influence on a global scale would be relatively limited for the foreseeable future. Tellingly, it was at precisely this moment that an interest in what was then termed "overseas heritage" emerged in Dutch government circles, beginning with the publicized concern of some center-right politicians for the decaying state of VOC cemeteries along India's coastline. Over the course of the 1990s and early 2000s, such overseas heritage—which was gradually rechristened "mutual," "shared," or "common" heritage—attracted increasing attention from the Dutch public and private sectors. While at this point not yet articulated as formal policy, the practice of government bodies offering financial support to initiatives led by Dutch heritage professionals working in former colonies and other past mercantile outposts became routine. As described to me by the director of CIE (the Center for International Heritage Activities, a quasi-private organization initially established in large part to coordinate MCH projects), the practice of this proto-policy was notable for its fluidity and ad hoc nature. A maritime archaeologist who was excavating VOC shipwrecks in Sri Lanka when the Hague first started to show interest in such activities as "mutual cultural heritage,"

he recalled that researchers were afforded significant leeway to do with this funding as they saw fit, the only demands placed on them by the Dutch government being the general stipulation that they contribute to the building of positive relations with counterparts in the country "hosting" this heritage.

Starting in 2009, the promotion of mutual cultural heritage became an official policy of the Dutch government, designed by the Ministries of Foreign Affairs and Education, Culture, and Science, and implemented by a range of public, private, and public-private organizations. The result, as one might expect, was to make the newly articulated MCH Programme a more formalized affair. From now on, MCH activities would be focused on eight "priority countries" that were designated by the Dutch state as possessing significant mutual cultural heritage due to a history of prolonged contact with the Netherlands: at first, these were Indonesia, Suriname, South Africa, India, Sri Lanka, Russia, Brazil, and Ghana. Funding also became more regimented at this time, distributed not directly to professionals or organizations but channeled instead through Dutch embassies in the priority countries. Also, the principle of matching funds became of central importance; the Netherlands would finance up to 60 percent of projects, while local partners would be expected to pick up the rest of the bill. While opinions on this newly formalized policy framework vary, a common criticism is that these two changes in the structure of mutual cultural heritage funding have led to smaller-scale local heritage organizations being crowded out by more well-established players in the priority country's heritage network. From the perspective of the Dutch government however, this articulation of the MCH Programme was deemed a great success, and so was renewed for a second term of 2013 to 2016. Some minor changes have been made in this newest iteration. Most notably, the list of priority countries has been amended: Ghana has been dropped and the United States, Australia, and Japan added.[3]

Since the MCH Programme's formalization, numerous projects have been carried out in its name, including the renovation of buildings, the digitization of archives, the training of practitioners, and the designing of cultural tourism attractions. In fact, the popular policy shows little sign of stopping any time soon.

How Much Diplomacy and How Much Heritage?
The phenomenon of heritage diplomacy necessarily prompts the simple question of how much is concerned with heritage and how much with diplomacy. That is, to what degree does the cause of heritage function as merely convenient and attractive packaging for more immediate diplomatic agendas, both economic and political? Or, the reverse, to what degree does the substance and specifics of the heritage in question itself

capture the attention of the governments involved or direct the course of their diplomatic relations? Of course, the dutiful anthropologist would reply that the reality is surely some mixture of the two, though the precise heritage-to-diplomacy ratio is a matter that must be worked out on a case-by-case basis. In the case of the MCH Programme, I will argue that the Dutch government's policy is at once concerned with pragmatic demands of international relations in the present and fundamentally shaped by the very history it purports to preserve.

Diplomacy

Indeed, in several respects, heritage has by no means been the priority of the Mutual Cultural Heritage Programme. Rather, the Dutch government has used the cause of heritage protection and cultural promotion as a channel (less generously put, as an excuse) through which to pursue the present-day interests of the Netherlands vis-à-vis other nations it considers of immediate political and economic import, with relatively weaker regard for the actual content of that history or eventual fate of the cultural property that recalls it.

This pragmatic emphasis on the diplomacy side of heritage diplomacy is evident in multiple aspects of the MCH Programme's planning and implementation. To begin, the authors of the latest version of the policy are quite up front about its primary objective, as evident in their brief on the 2013–2016 renewal: "International collaboration in the area of shared cultural heritage offers opportunities for the Netherlands. It can, for instance, oil the wheels of public and economic diplomacy."[4]

Moving from words to actions, another clear indication of the core priorities of the MCH Programme is simply the aforementioned revision of "priority countries" that came with the policy's latest extension. Tellingly, Ghana was dropped, and the United States, Japan, and Australia added. In discussions with employees at CIE who had previously worked on the several MCH projects in Ghana, it was stressed that the day-to-day logistical and bureaucratic complications of doing heritage work in that country were deemed by Dutch policymakers as just not worth the potential improvement in bilateral relations. Simply stated, the strategic political and economic use of Ghana to the Netherlands is far outranked by that of the United States, Japan, and Australia. Moreover, one cannot help but notice that the nature the Netherlands' past interactions with these newly listed priority countries highlights a history significantly less sensitive than the history of the Dutch in Ghana, with controversial sites like Elmina Castle necessarily drawing attention to the WIC's involvement in the transatlantic slave trade.

2. Exhibitions at the Tropenmuseum, Amsterdam, in 2010. Photograph by Ziko van Dijk, Wikimedia, CC BY-SA 3.0 (https://commons.wikimedia.org/wiki /File:2010-01_Tropenmuseum.JPG).

Finally, there is the fact that the recent decision of the Ministry of Foreign Affairs to renew, and indeed to expand, the MCH Programme abroad was set against a backdrop of deep cuts in the public funding available to the heritage sector within the Netherlands itself. Targeted in particular were the institutions that curated tangible testaments to the nation's colonial past, including the Tropenmuseum (or Museum of the Tropics), the KIT (the Royal Institute for the Tropics), and the KITLV (the Royal Institute of Caribbean and Southeast Asian Studies).[5]

These institutions, which together house many of the artifacts, libraries, and archives produced by centuries of Dutch colonialism, were threatened with brutal staff cuts, truncated programs, and even complete closure. Ultimately, after a passionate campaign in both the Netherlands and overseas, these three organizations narrowly avoided complete dismantlement; nevertheless, in July 2013 the KIT library and archive were shut down, in June 2014 the KITLV's library and reading room were closed, and recently the Tropenmuseum has been compelled to merge with two other museums dedicated to the "non-West" (the Volkenkunde Museum and the Afrika Museum) in order to stay afloat.[6]

While the public budgets for international cultural policy and these heritage institutions in the Netherlands were not technically linked—it was not as if the Ministry of Foreign

Affairs siphoned off funding for the Tropenmuseum directly into the coffers of the MCH Programme—the broader irony, one might say hypocrisy, that the Dutch government saw fit to cut support for preserving the testaments to its colonial past at home while simultaneously expanding its encouragement of such activities abroad was not lost on interested observers at the time. Tellingly, some of the loudest cries of protest came from scholars based in the priority countries who actually used the resources of the Tropenmuseum, KIT, and KITLV on a regular basis to conduct research into the history of their own nations. Indeed, in this sense the reading room of an archive in Leiden or the gallery space of a museum in Amsterdam, where on any given day Indonesian, South African, and Dutch researchers could be found working side-by-side or deep in conversation, represented a far more "mutual" cultural heritage than a crumbling fort on some distant shore that might be visited by only a handful of (largely foreign) tourists. The conclusion drawn by many onlookers in the heritage community, which I heard articulated in public workshops and private conversations in both the Netherlands and Indonesia during the height of this crisis, was that the Dutch government evidently possessed little in the way of genuine concern for heritage itself, being primarily motivated in its policy decisions by the present-day political and economic possibilities that heritage *diplomacy* could offer.

Heritage

However, parallel to this fact that the Netherlands' support of mutual cultural heritage abroad is undoubtedly undergirded by immediate and pragmatic geopolitical self-interest, there is also evidence for this policy being itself shaped in significant part by the very history that it purports to preserve. By this I mean that particular characteristics of Dutch colonialism, especially in the nineteenth and early twentieth centuries, can be seen to have influenced not only the rather singular attitude of contemporary Dutch society towards that past, but also to have echoes in the premise and practice of the MCH Programme.

Consider the language of "mutual," "shared," and "common" that pervades the policy. In truth, the relevant Dutch term is *gemeenschappelijk cultureel erfgoed,* but in practice the great majority of the government briefs, project reviews, and memoranda of understanding are written entirely in English, where this phrase is translated into these three aforementioned words almost interchangeably, or, "at random" as one Dutch curator once said with some exasperation.[7] In this article, only the "mutual cultural heritage" nomenclature is used in part for simplicity's sake but also because this was the initial term suggested in 1988 by Indonesia's then Minister of Culture as an alternative to "colonial heritage."[8] Interestingly, while it was a representative from a former colony who first articulated this concept, it was the Dutch who then ran with it (the Indonesians having lost much of their appetite for such shows of bilateral coziness after a series of diplomatic snafus made for a chilly relationship with the Netherlands for most of the 1990s). As the concept of mutual cultural heritage gained traction within the Hague over the next few years, Dutch heritage professionals also began to popularize the concept widely in their own circles, for instance by inaugurating and chairing the ICOMOS International Scientific Committee on Shared Colonial Architecture and Town Planning in 1998 (later renamed the ISC on Shared Built Heritage in 2003, after pressure from politicians to drop the "Colonial" altogether). It was the Netherlands, then, that was in fact largely responsible for *mutual, shared,* and *common* becoming buzzwords of international heritage discourse in the early 2000s.

While this terminology has been criticized even by some of its own advocates as being so vague as to be virtually unworkable, it nevertheless possesses a political power — or rather, a power to depoliticize. As has likely become clear by now, *mutual, shared,* or *common* are not adjectives that emerged in isolation; instead, they were from the very start deployed as more benign replacements for that far riskier word, *colonial.* Not surprisingly, however, this attempt to dull the barb of that original term has not been universally embraced. Within the Netherlands, heritage professionals from both sides of the political spectrum took issue, those more conservatively minded dismissing the new terminology as one more example of political correctness gone too far, and those more progressively inclined taking issue with it for precluding any kind of substantive dialogue on the uncomfortable truths of colonialism. Those in the MCH priority countries were also skeptical — in virtually every report of the many Heritage Days (which are CIE-led conferences where representatives from the Netherlands and the priority country first meet), the point is raised again and again that the "mutual" in "mutual cultural heritage" is problematic. To some, a Dutch fort is Dutch heritage, not "mutual"; to others, any objects or structures that fall within a nation's borders are necessarily the patrimony of that nation (again, not "mutual"). Or, as perceptively put by one Indonesian audience member at a 2011 conference presentation that cast the Volkenkunde Museum's ethnographic collections as "shared heritage," "Since these objects were all created by Indonesians, how do you call this 'shared'?"[9]

Beneath this disagreement over the precise borders of *mutual, shared,* and *common* as labels for actual historical materials or sites, there is also the more profound point that such words are simply inappropriate to apply to colonial, and indeed postcolonial contexts, because that brutal history was by its very nature neither mutual, shared, nor common. As articulated so well by Alex van Stipriaan, a former curator at the Tropenmuseum, "The problem is that all heritages we are talking about here are related to the history of European expansion and colonialism and therefore subject from the beginning to a-symmetrical power relations . . . Historical synchronicity in time and space should not be confused with mutuality . . . [in MCH activities] the parties involved more often than not do NOT constitute a community, they are NOT equals, for instance when it comes to finances, and they DON'T always share or have a share."[10]

Despite the obviously problematic nature of *mutual, shared,* and *common,* and the fact that some heritage professionals, both foreign and Dutch, have taken issue with their use, this terminology has stuck in the Netherlands. The reasons for its persistence are many, but two especially stand out: First, the apoliticism of such a discourse harmonizes with the broader attitudes of contemporary Dutch society, in which the majority of people give little thought to the colonial past and, when they do, tend to perceive this history as benign (or even as a source of pride) and its legacies as inconsequential.[11] Indeed, the kinds of impassioned debates over colonialism and its legacies that have taken place in the Anglo- and Francophone worlds have simply not yet emerged in the Netherlands,[12] where many scholars and ordinary people alike see the Dutch empire as qualitatively different from its British and French parallels — less ideologically motivated from the start, less destructive in the past, less relevant in the present.[13] While this attitude has been slowly changing in recent years — today it would be unlikely that the kind of tone-deaf celebrations of the VOC's four hundredth anniversary that were held in 2002 would be repeated — such a perception of Dutch colonialism still persists even in more progressive circles. For example, in 2012 a critically acclaimed documentary film installation was produced that revisited the landscapes where Dutch merchants and colonizers once tread. An otherwise perceptive and moving piece, its title was rather predictable: *Empire: The Unintended Consequences of Dutch Colonialism,* as if colonialism and its legacies were mere happenstance.

This contemporary attitude toward the colonial past did not just emerge out of thin air. Indeed, the second reason why the language of *mutual, shared,* and *common* still has such strong currency in the Netherlands is that, historically, it functioned as a key element of the carefully constructed self-image of the Dutch empire, especially in the late nineteenth and

3. VOC-themed souvenirs at the National Maritime Museum in Amsterdam. Courtesy of the author.

early twentieth centuries. Take, for instance, the case of the late colonial Dutch East Indies, today the Republic of Indonesia. In a 1901 speech, the Dutch Queen Willhelmina formally announced the inauguration of a new direction in the administration of her Southeast Asian colony: the Ethical Policy. In its most general sense, the Ethical Policy was the Netherlands' version of Britain's "white man's burden" or France's *mission civilisatrice,* a rerouting of colonial governance intended to bring the great watchword of that time — "progress" — to the archipelago.[14] This would be achieved through the purported "modernization" of the colony in the fields of health and hygiene, urban planning, infrastructure, education, and so on. Such modernization would be orchestrated by an army of experts, or what one historian calls "a technical intelligentsia [who] had the final say."[15] Aware of parallel modernizing initiatives being carried out by their European rivals in their own colonies, proponents of the Ethical Policy sought to distinguish the Dutch approach from that of the British or French by casting those as mere brute impositions of Western knowledge and technologies upon an unprepared local population. Rather, the Dutch colonizers in their presentation of the Ethical Policy (if not in their execution of it) made much of their ability to put their advanced "anthropological learning and greater cultural sensitivity" to work in modernizing the lives of their subjects in a fashion keeping with their own indigenous culture (as identified by Dutch experts).[16] The intended result of this apparently

4. The 1938 triptych by H. Paulides at the KIT headquarters in Amsterdam representing "het Westen" (the West) as scientific research and engineering works, "het Oosten" (the East) as agricultural labor and cultural pastimes, and "de Samenwerking" (Cooperation) as a harmonious blending of the two (*top*). In a detail of "de Samenwerking" panel, a Dutch engineer and his Indonesian colleague (assistant?) look over blueprints for new irrigation infrastructure while surrounded by symbols of Eastern tradition and Western modernity (*bottom*). Photographs by Kris Roderburg, Rijksdienst voor het Cultureel Erfgoed, CC BY-SA 3.0 NL.

more sophisticated—and beneficent—approach to empire
was to be a hybridized society, something uniquely "Indies":
modernity and tradition, East and West, brought together not
in conflict but in *samenwerking* or "cooperation."

At the time, this rosy discourse was perhaps no more
literally put on display than at the 1931 Colonial Exhibition in
Paris.[17] Here, the Netherlands' pavilion—an enormous construction that blended together vernacular architectural motifs
from around the Indonesian archipelago and infused them with
the sensibilities of the latest movements in Dutch modernist
design[18]—stood out starkly from the staged "native" villages
and reconstructed streetscapes of its British and French
counterparts.

As the Dutch historian Frances Gouda explains, this effort to creatively synthesize "East" and "West" was explicitly
intended as further evidence of the successes of Dutch "enlightened" and "progressive" rule in the colony, which could
claim to have distilled and enhanced (not merely copied or
preserved) some core quality of its indigenous subjects.

When seen in light of the contemporary matter of the MCH
Programme, here in the late colonial Dutch East Indies we can
see a precedent being set for a self-consciously apolitical por-
trayal of the colonial experience as one characterized by mutuality, sharing, and commonality, not domination, violence, and
paternalism. Moreover, this earlier narrative was intended not
only for the domestic consumption of a Dutch public but also
as part of a broader geopolitical strategy for the "diminutive
democracy" of the Netherlands to distinguish itself in relation to its more powerful European neighbors. Their purported
pursuit of an enlightened approach to the imperial game would
cast these Dutch colonizers as "governing their districts with
more anthropological learning, greater cultural sensitivity, and
better political skills than any other imperial power in Asia." In
short, as Gouda again explains, the Dutch would "employ the
ingenuity of David in order to maintain themselves among the
Goliaths of Empire."[19]

To conclude on an intriguing aside, this is precisely the
approach that the contemporary Netherlands still takes regarding the part it has chosen to play in the wider geopolitical
arena. Knowing that it has at its disposal neither the money
nor the manpower of, say, a United Kingdom or a France to
pursue projects abroad, the Dutch state has actively sought
to cultivate instead a global reputation for bringing an especially high level of experience, skills, and ideas to its overseas
initiatives. That is, to punch above its proverbial weight in the
international ring, the Netherlands has strategically cast itself
as a nation of brains over brawn. This official promotion of
Dutch expertise overseas has, on a discursive level at least, the

5. The pavilion representing the Dutch East Indies at the 1931 Exposition Coloniale in Paris, exterior (*top*) and interior (*bottom*). Courtesy of Leiden University Library (image codes 1406835 and 1403950).

same effect of earlier, colonial-era moves of the same ilk: that is, to cast the actions of the Dutch state abroad as apolitical (being objective interventions based on technical know-how) and beneficent (being motivated by humanitarian aims). Thus, when the MCH Programme deploys the language of heritage "expertise" (which it does with almost the same frequency of that intimately related terminology of *mutual, shared,* and *common*), it is again participating in a contemporary discourse that serves present-day political aims but is itself also steeped in historical precedent.

One could not blame the ambitious van Overvoorde—
or the architects of the Mutual Cultural Heritage Programme
decades later—for wanting to make known to the wider world
the expansive reach and lasting legacies of the Dutch empire.
Indeed, the postcolonial Netherlands is chronically overlooked
in scholarly discussions that usually focus on the activities
of greater geopolitical heavyweights or the legacies of more
widely studied former empires. This article has sought to demonstrate that turning our attention to this deceptively "diminutive" nation, and to the societies, near and far, it once sought
to rule over, has the potential to reveal many insights.

Specifically with regards to the case of the MCH Programme
presented here, two wider lessons emerge. First, while it is crucial that we give attention to the increasing exercise of heritage
diplomacy by states belonging broadly to the "non-West" (as
do other authors, with great sensitivity and rigor, in this issue),
it is equally crucial that we do not as a result homogenize "the
West" in our analyses, but rather recognize the great diversity
of approaches to international cultural policy that exist within
such a heavily constructed category. Second, in our exploration of this contemporary phenomenon, we must remember the
seemingly self-evident (but in fact oft-forgotten) point that history, or rather historical specificity, matters. Heritage diplomacy
today is of course driven in part by the political and economic
forces of the moment, but it is also shaped by forces of the past.
Clearly, the case of heritage diplomacy in the contemporary
Netherlands emphasizes the importance of steering clear of an
assumed, over-generalized colonial experience (or indeed, a
postcolonial one) in scholarly analyses, and instead to give serious consideration to the specificities and even idiosyncrasies of
different imperial histories. That is, while I have refrained from
characterizing the MCH Programme as "neocolonial" (believ-
ing that that terminology prematurely closes off more paths of
inquiry than it opens), I am proposing that there is a reason,
and a distinctly *historical* reason, why the language of *mutual,
shared,* and *common* (along with its close companion, *expertise*) has been taken up with gusto in the Dutch context, and
why such a discourse appears to gain traction in some overseas
settings but not in others. Indeed, I would go so far as to posit
that in our emerging field of heritage studies, we often become
so concerned with understanding how the present influences
our view of the past that we risk losing sight of that past itself.

Biography
Lauren Yapp is a PhD candidate in the Anthropology Department at Stanford University and recipient of a 2014–2015 Fulbright research grant. Her doctoral fieldwork
examines public, private, and community efforts to preserve the historical fabric
of Indonesia's urban centers, and in particular the transnational/postcolonial networks that form around such heritage-related initiatives in the cities of Semarang,
Bandung, and Jakarta.

Notes

The author would like to thank Tim Winter and her fellow panelists at the 2014 Association of Critical Heritage Studies conference for their insights on and enthusiasm for the topic of heritage diplomacy. She is also grateful to the Stanford Archaeology Center, the Stanford Anthropology Department, and the Fulbright Program for the funding that has made her fieldwork in Indonesia and the Netherlands possible. Mas Yogi took time out of his own busy schedule to provide assistance with images and formatting, *terima kasih*. And lastly, many thanks to Lynn Meskell, Wim Manuhutu, and Pauline van Roosmalen for their advice, clarifications, and encouragements regarding this article at various points over the course of its development.

[1] In the original Dutch: "Want Overvoorde was allerminst een vlot en gemakkelijk man . . . de trouw aan het aangenomen beginsel . . . doorzettingsvermogen . . . plichtsgetrouwe arbeidzaamheid, dat nooit aflatend werken, die in het aangezicht van den dood zelfs onbreekbare hardnekkigheid . . . ." H. E. van Gelder, "Levensbericht van Mr Dr J C Overvoorde," in *Jaarboek van de Maatschappij der Nederlandse Letterkunde over het jaar 1929–1930,* 70–90 (Leiden: E. J. Brill, 1930), 71.

[2] A. Fienieg, R. Parthesius, B. Groot, R. Jaffe, S. van der Linde, and P. van Roosmalen, "Heritage Tails: International Cultural Heritage Policies in a European Perspective," in *Dutch Colonialism, Migration, and Cultural Heritage,* ed. G. Oostindie, 23–62 (Leiden: Brill, 2008), 23.

[3] E. Smid and P. van Eersel, *Mid-term Review GCE-beleid* (2012) 353980, available at: https://www.rijksoverheid.nl/documenten/rapporten/2012/09/07/mid-term-review-gce-beleid; *Shared Cultural Heritage Policy Framework 2013–2016* (2012), AVT12/BZ107098, available at: http://en.nationaalarchief.nl/sites/default/files/docs/gce_beleidskader_2013-2016_definitief_-_eng_doca.pdf.

[4] *Shared Cultural Heritage Policy Framework 2013–2016,* 3.

[5] While the cuts to each of these institutions were formally overseen by different government departments, they occurred at the same time and in the same spirit, and so were perceived by scholars and employees as part of a single, wider policy for the scaling back (or even dismantling) of government support for the study and discussion of Dutch colonialism.

[6] During the preparation of this article, it was announced that, as part of this merger, the Tropenmuseum will receive additional funding through the Ministry of Education, Culture, and Science that will ease its operating costs for the foreseeable future.

[7] A. van Stipriaan, "Atlantic Heritage: Mutual, Shared . . . ?" Conference proceedings of *Atlantic World and the Dutch,* November 27–December 12, 2006, Amsterdam, The Netherlands.

[8] C. Min Chin, *Memory Contested, Locality Transformed: Representing Japanese Colonial "Heritage" in Taiwan,"* PhD Diss., Leiden University, the Netherlands, 2012, 17.

[9] Quoted in ibid., 21.

[10] Van Stipriaan, "Atlantic Heritage," emphasis in original.

[11] E. Boehmer and S. de Mul, "Introduction," in *The Postcolonial Low Countries: Literature, Colonialism, and Multiculturalism,* ed. Boehmer and de Mul, 1–22 (Lanham, Md.: Lexington Books, 2012); U. Bosma, "Why Is There No Post-colonial Debate in the Netherlands?" in *Post-colonial Immigrants and Identity Formations in the Netherlands,* ed. Bosma (Amsterdam: Amsterdam University Press, 2012); A. Smits, "The Netherlands in Post-colonial Perspective: Compared with Other European Art Institutes, Those in the Netherlands Lag Behind in Processing their Nation's Colonial Past," *Metropolis M* 5 (October/November 2011): http://metropolism.com/magazine/2011-no5/niet-willen-weten/english.

[12] Boehmer and de Mul summarize well this lack of attention to postcolonial themes in mainstream Dutch cultural and intellectual discourse: "This writing off . . . is predicated on postcolonial concepts being taken as in some sense 'foreign,' borrowed or non-native, something that doesn't suit us, or, alternatively, that we don't adequately do, or aren't equal to. This too-ready Dutch acceptance of belatedness vis-à-vis the postcolonial, [is] at times [met] with an almost audible exclamation of relief . . . Ah, the resolutely non-postcolonial Dutch culture critic sighs, we don't need to be bothering with that colonial-type business after all. It is past its sell-by date ("Introduction," 8)."

[13] For an example of this position, as taken by the director of the KITLV, see G. Oostindie, *Postcolonial Netherlands: Sixty-five Years of Forgetting, Commemorating, Silencing* (Amsterdam: Amsterdam University Press, 2011).

[14] W. Ravesteijn, "Between Globalisation and Localisation: The Case of Dutch Civil Engineering in Indonesia, 1800–1950," *Comparative Technology Transfer and Society* 5, no. 1 (2007): 32–65 at 37; T. Li, *The Will to Improve: Governmentality, Development, and the Practice of Politics* (Durham, N.C.: Duke University Press, 2007), 32.

15 J. van Doorn, *The Engineers and the Colonial System: Technocratic Tendencies in the Dutch East Indies* (Rotterdam: Comparative Asian Studies Program, 1982), 28.
16 F. Gouda, *Dutch Culture Overseas: Colonial Practice in the Netherlands East Indies* (Sheffield, U.K: Equinox, 1995), 41.
17 Ibid.; M. van Bloembergen, *Colonial Spectacles: The Netherlands and the Netherlands–Indies at the World Exhibitions, 1880–1931* (Singapore: NUS Press, 2009).
18 Gouda, *Dutch Culture Overseas*, 210–13.
19 Ibid., 41.

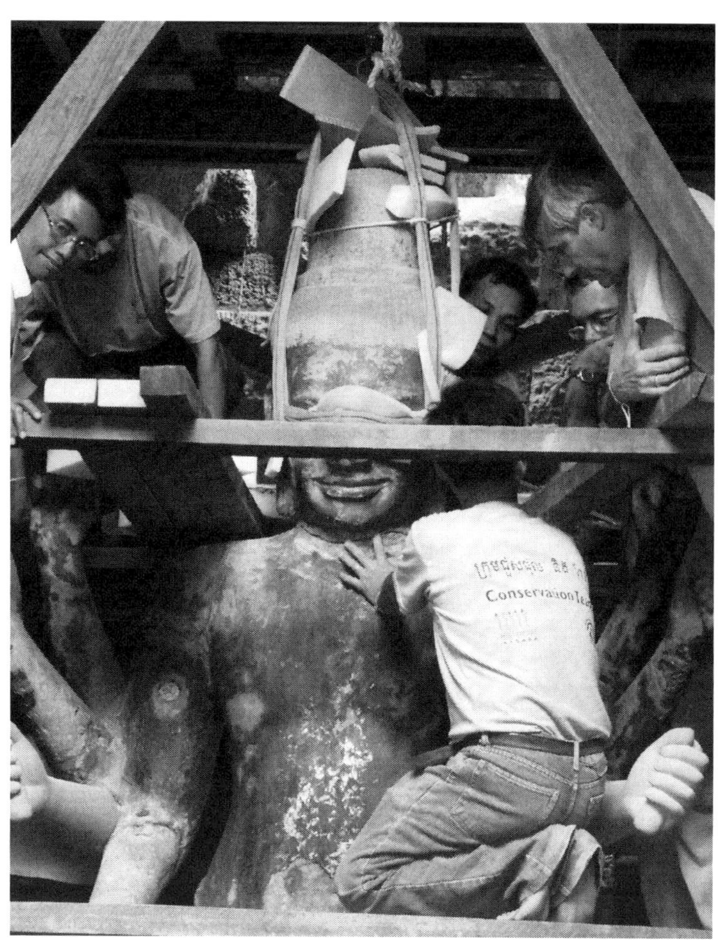

1. Restoration of Ta Reach, Angkor Wat, Cambodia. Photograph by T. Winter.

Luke James

The Symbolic Value of Expertise in International Heritage Diplomacy

International historic preservation may conjure images of teams of preservation experts on the ground working at a site such as Angkor, Cambodia, rather than in air-conditioned conference centers. Yet this privileging of the photogenic material preservation object may obscure other, less commonly recognized aspects of the international preservation regime. This includes multilateral governance arenas where policy is set and decisions are made, such as the UNESCO World Heritage Committee. The role of preservation experts in the former setting appears self-evident, needing only images of the expert, tool in hand, or perhaps before-and-after photographs, to establish that preservation is being done. This powerful site-based symbolism drives the publicity of organizations such as the World Monuments Fund and has also been a major factor in attracting a diverse group of national governments to use preservation projects as an outlet for international diplomacy, from the U.S. archaeological work abroad as an avenue of foreign policy[1] to the Chinese government's multimillion dollar preservation at Chao Say Tevoda, Angkor.[2] However, critical attention has also turned to the diplomacy implicit in the policy and decision-making processes within the global governance of historic preservation.[3] The diplomatic potential of both settings has given rise to the concept of heritage diplomacy.[4]

Like site-based preservation, the international governance of historic preservation deploys technical advice and advisers styled as specifically preservation expertise and experts — architects, archaeologists, conservators, historians, and others. But unlike site-based preservation, in this forum the work of these technical preservation experts is frequently performed far from the preservation object — in reports, presentations to decision-makers, and backroom meetings. Here I wish to cast light on the work of technical preservation experts away from the preservation object, and use the concept of heritage diplomacy to frame these lesser-known practices. In doing so I will use the example of the UNESCO World Heritage system, perhaps the site par excellence for the study of both heritage diplomacy and expertise. As Tim Winter argues, World Heritage encourages nations to be internationally disposed, and opens up new and important forms of soft diplomacy resting upon long-standing structures of international cooperation.[5] Expertise is structured into the negotiated decisions that form the

Future Anterior
Volume XIII, Number 1
Summer 2016

subject of diplomatic practice at the annual meetings of the World Heritage Committee. However, compared with its prominent use in depictions of onsite practices in contact with the preservation object, when structured into forms recognizable to bureaucratic or political decision-making, as can be seen in the World Heritage Committee, the symbolic value of technical preservation expertise as such is reduced. Yet this also has the perhaps unexpected effect of making such knowledge easier to circulate in negotiations that constitute an important aspect of heritage diplomacy in that forum.

The Status of Expertise in Historic Preservation

A useful starting point here is to consider what comprises specific technical expertise in historic preservation. Historic preservation practice is multidisciplinary, involving professions, trades, as well as customary knowledge and practice. Aside from architects' involvement, historic preservation is not generally subject to professional entry limitations, or minimum academic levels (such as in the sciences). However, preservation may involve restrictions on trades appellations (stonemasons, for example, may need to hold a license to call themselves stonemasons) and rules or laws within cultural groups that govern who has the right to enter, touch, or perform work on particular places. Increasingly, traditional practicing disciplines and trades associated with historic preservation (architects, archaeologists, historians, materials conservators, stonemasons, carpenters, etc.) are now joined by engineers, laboratory scientists, academics, project managers, town and transport planners, and others who (with no disrespect—I too share this background) can only be grouped together as functional specialists in various instruments of preservation governance, including national or international civil servants and staff in the secretariats of professional historic preservation organizations.

I argue there are two broad typologies that can be superimposed on these areas of expert involvement in historic preservation. The first, following Winter and Muñoz Viñas, I refer to as materiality, "where the expert professional is defined by two factors: close physical proximity to the object and a 'strongly specific knowledge'."[6] This invokes the traditional practicing conservation disciplines and trades, who work on—uncover, categorize, date, form, re-form, smell, and touch—historic fabric or, to be agnostic to the hegemonic categories of heritage or historic preservation, what Denis Byrne usefully terms "old places and things."[7] Reflecting this involvement, the expert knowledge they produce may tend toward the scientistic materialism identified by Winter as an epistemological bias in the preservation sector.[8] While recognizing the large body of examples of reflexive and critical practice by those engaged in this category, by and large this epistemological focus has been an obstacle to connecting such practice to

> the various ways in which heritage now has a stake in, and can act as a positive enabler for, the complex, multi-vector challenges that face us today, such as cultural and environmental sustainability, economic inequalities, conflict resolution, social cohesion and the future of cities, to name a few.[9]

The second broad typology is bureaucracy. This is not limited to the officials serving as functional specialists in instruments of historic preservation governance that might invoke Weber,[10] but all those that claim a place in such governance but lack a claim to "close physical proximity to the object." What distinguishes this type of practice is that it is frequently channeled through a governance structure or aesthetic that shapes the outputs of the work to the needs of that governance structure, typically the acts of writing and reporting, with the clearest example perhaps the "desktop review"—technical preservation advice provided absent the physical presence of a site or object. However, it also includes the many forms of management planning—from management of preservation, to tourism and even transport—that are now seen as routine elements of a holistic approach to preservation governance. This is demonstrated, for example, in the decisions adopted by the World Heritage Committee as recommended by its historic preservation adviser, ICOMOS.[11] For example, the decision to inscribe the Japanese Sites of the Meiji Industrial Revolution included recommendations that, among other things, Japan: develop as a priority a detailed conservation work program and an implementation program (preservation planning); define acceptable visitor threshold levels (tourism planning); establish and implement an ongoing training program for all staff (vocational training); and submit all development projects for road construction projects and for a new anchorage facility to the World Heritage Committee for examination (transport planning).[12]

Here we see how recognition of a large preservation object (in this case, a grouping of eleven sites spread across Japan) gives rise to a spread of potential issues of concern and requires a larger and more diverse set of disciplines as well as public and private entities to be involved. This contrasts with the traditional preservation object of the "monument" around which scientific materialism became ordered (for example, see the Venice Charter).[13] However, it also reflects a structuring

2. Aerial view of the Hashima coal mine, part of the Sites of Japan's Meiji Industrial Revolution. Copyright Nagasaki Prefecture.

of the expert knowledge provided by the "preservation expert" into governance instruments and normative practice through which this hybrid preservation expert–bureaucrat practice becomes consolidated and durable.

The status of the expert and of expertise in historic preservation has historically received little attention, but this field of research is starting to grow. Critical attention is turning to historic preservation experts working with communities in the field and in the decision-making centers of global historic preservation governance such as the World Heritage Committee and other UNESCO cultural conventions.[14] These accounts share an essential ambivalence about the role of expertise in historic preservation practice and governance. For Walker, expertise is a relational concept, with an expert being someone successfully socialized into the domain of expertise and able to cite others in the discipline who support his or her view.[15] Walker thereby argues for a more critically reflexive consideration of what constitutes preservation expertise and a collaborative, facilitative role in their work in communities.

More cynically, Lixinski traces the role of preservation expertise in the framing of legal structures of international preservation, and particularly the UNESCO cultural conventions and their antecedents. As argued by Lixinski, the people who

3. Preah Vihear Temple. Photograph by T. Winter.

shaped these instruments used their particular disciplinary backgrounds, and their forms of knowledge became centrally structured into these instruments, thus making their expertise synonymous with preservation expertise. As he puts it:

> Law drafted due to the encouragement of experts tends to rely on experts for its own drafting and, consequently, for its implementation, enabling experts to create self-perpetuating mechanisms to ensure their own relevance and the relevance of their espoused views.[16]

Of particular relevance to the relationship of expert knowledge to the practice of heritage diplomacy, Lixinski uses archival documents to trace how UNESCO's mandate in cultural preservation became "scientificised" into an apolitical field marshaled by neutral experts. This then became the avenue by which the preservation concept could become globalized through an international historic preservation system that, in turn, used this depoliticized, scientistic preservation concept to sidestep problematic international political and legal determinations about ownership, territory, and property.[17]

This last point may appear surprising in the light of recent international flashpoints coalescing around historic sites including Preah Vihear (between Cambodia and Thailand) and the World Heritage nomination (and subsequent listing) of the Japanese Sites of the Meiji Industrial Revolution, including sites associated with the World War II forced labor of Koreans and others.[18] But even here this might ignore the role of an

4. Preah Vihear Temple. Photograph by T. Winter.

expert historic preservation vocabulary to a diplomatic solution. For example, after high-level bilateral diplomatic and political negotiations, the denouement to the Japan–Korea dispute over the Meiji-era site centered on a familiar prescription of a preservation expert—an agreement by Japan to include mention of forced labor in onsite interpretation.[19]

James and Winter take a different approach, arguing for a broadening of the conceptual category of expert in international preservation governance, and in particular the World Heritage system, to include not just technical expertise but diplomatic and institutional forms of expertise.[20] Approaching expertise as an assemblage of forms, they argue, is a more productive way to better understand the dynamics of knowledge production in this area. In part, they argue that this involves performances of objectivity, familiar to the role of the technical expert, but also of cultural capital, such as linguistic virtuosity, more familiar to the diplomat, and knowledge of process and form, as demonstrated by the institutional expert—and that these are frequently blended in the one person.[21]

Moving outside preservation studies, the constitution of expert identity in international development is a focus of the work of Mosse.[22] Mosse's ethnographic work reads into the messiness of constructing and stabilizing both an identity as a professional development expert and "the universals of expert knowledge" in the face of "the unmanageability of the immediately local, of uncertainty and the risk of failure."[23] Mosse's particular insight is that expert knowledge, in order to be rec-

5. Preah Vihear Temple. Photograph by T. Winter.

ognized as such, is the product of a victorious struggle across numerous domains:

> Decision-making knowledge — even apparently hard economic facts and statistics — is produced out of complex relationships, contests over status, across different disciplinary points of view . . . that define what counts as knowledge.[24]

Some underlying themes can be discerned from these views on expert knowledge and expertise. It is now a mature observation from the literature on science and technology studies that the closer a researcher focuses on the day-to-day work of technical advisers — experts — and their products — expert knowledge — the less enchanted and more arbitrary it appears.[25] From this anthropological (and specifically ethnographic) viewpoint, the multidisciplinary nature of historic preservation practice appears particularly prone to the "contests over status, across different disciplinary points of view" that Mosse has observed. As Latour argues, durability does not lie in purely social explanations but rather in things, including pieces of paper. The structuring of expertise into global preservation governance instruments (such as the UNESCO cultural conventions) can be seen as providing some degree of durability to the experts' status in international preservation governance but, as we shall see in the example of the World Heritage Committee, this too is revealed as a subject of struggle.

The Bureaucratization of Expertise in World Heritage Decision Making

The UNESCO Convention concerning the protection of the world cultural and natural heritage (World Heritage Convention) was adopted in 1972 and came into force in 1975, with the objective of

> establishing an effective system of collective protection of the cultural and natural heritage of outstanding universal value, organized on a permanent basis and in accordance with modern scientific methods.[26]

Decisions under the Convention are made by a World Heritage Committee comprising delegates representing 21 of the (currently) 192 member states of the World Heritage Convention. It is most well known for creating the World Heritage List of places deemed to be of "outstanding universal value," having been adjudicated to have met one or more of ten criteria as well as integrity, authenticity (for cultural properties), and protection and management.[27] The most closely watched decisions of the World Heritage Committee during its annual meeting include decisions on inclusion or removal of a nominated place on the World Heritage List and decisions about the management and preservation of World Heritage sites. Sites remain under the jurisdiction of the state and their management remains the responsibility of the state apparatus, but decisions of the World Heritage Committee have weight because of the potential sanction of including a place on the List of World Heritage in Danger or removal from the list entirely. There are currently 1,052 places inscribed on the World Heritage List.

The World Heritage Committee is a very good example of how expert knowledge is structured into instruments of global heritage governance. Under the World Heritage Convention and its Operational Guidelines, states are required to "choose as their representatives persons qualified in the field of the cultural or natural heritage," while expert preservation bodies ICOMOS,[28] IUCN,[29] and ICCROM[30] have standing under the World Heritage Convention to attend meetings in an advisory capacity.[31] ICOMOS and IUCN in fact have a much more central role through the Operational Guidelines to the Convention. This includes responsibility for providing a technical assessment of nominations of sites, which, importantly, becomes the basis for the recommendation in the draft decision that forms the starting point of the World Heritage Committee's deliberations. It extends in practice also to providing the initial audio-visual presentation to the World Heritage Committee at the commencement of the discussion of each nomination. In this

6. Presentation from ICOMOS, 38th World Heritage Committee meeting, Doha, Qatar, 2014. Photograph by the author.

way, expert knowledge is structured into the decision-making process, framing the discussion that follows.

Despite this, Meskell and Bertacchini et al. have demonstrated that in recent years the decisions of the World Heritage Committee increasingly have been at odds with the recommendations of ICOMOS and, to a lesser extent, IUCN.[32] This culminated at the Doha World Heritage Committee meeting in 2014 with 47 percent of ICOMOS and IUCN recommendations being overturned.[33] The result has been an accelerating rate of inscriptions in cases where ICOMOS and IUCN urged the need for further work. Meskell et al. question whether "technical aspects like conservation or management are still paramount or whether member countries' special interests and their lobby groups have major influence," and link this phenomenon to a change in the composition of the World Heritage Committee over time, which tipped the balance of power toward "BRICs" states.[34] They also point to similar trends more broadly in other intergovernmental bodies. As summarized by Bertacchini et al.,

> In such a politicized context, and with the allegedly increased disconnection of World Heritage Committee decisions from technical expertise, the main implication is that a State Party's nomination activity is more likely to act as a proxy for its strategic political influence and power within the multilateral system.[35]

7. Name plates from 39th World Heritage Committee meeting, Bonn 2015. Photograph by the author.

I want to take the discussion in a slightly different direction by returning to the typologies of materiality and bureaucracy. Here I argue that the structured practice of expertise at the World Heritage Committee as represented by ICOMOS is tempered into a bureaucratic register, a long way from its site-based practice and representation as materiality. In this setting, it becomes recognizable as a species of the bureaucratic and political decisions, which the diplomatic delegates representing states treat as their metier. This contributes to the World Heritage Committee as a site of diplomacy—a specific heritage diplomacy—because it enables those with diplomatic expertise (and here I do not mean only diplomats) to broker in this technical expertise as it becomes convertible as diplomatic currency.

There is a range of types of expert knowledge that flow through the World Heritage system, even if we restrict this to technical preservation knowledge, but in the space available here I will limit my focus to the work of ICOMOS in particular and its role in evaluating World Heritage nominations. ICOMOS has a normative process that is set out in an often-displayed flowchart—the flowchart being among perhaps the purest expressions of the aesthetic of bureaucratic practice—which typically includes both a desktop review of the often lengthy nomination dossier submitted by the nominating state and other information, followed by a site visit coordinated by the nominating state. This culminates in a report considered by an annual ICOMOS "World Heritage Panel" meeting in ICOMOS's Paris headquarters and ultimately finalized into ICOMOS's official advice to the World Heritage Committee.

As the excerpt from the Japanese Sites of the Meiji Industrial Revolution demonstrated—along with an evaluation of significance against criteria, integrity, and authenticity—ICOMOS's technical preservation advice also moves into areas more clearly governmental and even political in nature, including governance and legislative arrangements. Further examples can be found from ICOMOS's advice to the 2014 and 2015 World Heritage Committee meetings. In relation to the La Rioja and Rioja Alavesa Wine and Vineyard Cultural Landscape (Spain), ICOMOS wrote that it "considers that the management system for the property will be adequate when the bilateral protocols between La Rioja and the Basque Country are signed."[36] ICOMOS also makes recommendations that touch on how a state governs its citizens, though in language crafted to adhere to its technical mandate. ICOMOS may, for instance, comment on the level of consultation or otherwise of communities living in and around a site, or even on issues as politically sensitive as community relocation. For example, ICOMOS recommended that inscription of the Barotse Cultural Landscape (Zambia) be deferred to a future meeting, recommending that "management needs to be more participatory in involving local communities."[37] In its assessment of the nomination of the Tusi Sites (China), ICOMOS noted a reference to funds set aside for future relocation of residents to facilitate tourism, surveying, and archaeological excavations and responded that "the relocation of inhabitants is not necessary to sustain the conservation of the property."[38]

The argument here is not that the technical/political dichotomy in global governance is unstable, that the technical can mean political by other means, or that preservation practice has inescapably political dimensions. All of these arguments have been strongly made elsewhere and need not be repeated here. Rather, I wish to provide an account as to how expert practices in global governance of historic preservation facilitate preservation as a vehicle for this diplomacy. In this case, recalling how Meskell has demonstrated that the World Heritage Committee is increasingly overturning the advice of its expert bodies, especially ICOMOS, I add the observation that this may be connected to the way in which expert knowledge is tempered into a bureaucratic register. Of course, much of the technical advice of expert bodies is much closer to the materialist than bureaucratic registers, for example where it assesses authenticity based on stylistic considerations, or recommends a particular preservation treatment to a component. However, to the degree that it also includes advice on matters recognizable to bureaucratic administration or political decision-making, such as transport planning, citizen involvement, or occupancy rights, these practices of expertise become immediately relatable to the exercise of bureaucratic and political functions of states, as ultimate decision makers. Entering this register means that such knowledge competes with other relatable considerations — here I argue diplomatic considerations — and may be traded off accordingly.

By contrast, I see evidence of a foregrounding of a materialist technical expertise in the construction of preservation aid as diplomacy. Winter has traced the historical origins and contemporary practices of preservation assistance as a form of international aid. At a time when aid is increasingly seen as political, he has detected a "cultural turn" in which historic preservation becomes an attractive and apparently apolitical space for aid, which, nevertheless, remains a mechanism of soft power.[39] However, to function as such, I argue that in preservation aid as diplomacy it is the bolstering of the symbolic value of the involvement of experts that enables such assistance to secure the distance from political and economic spheres needed to function effectively as cultural diplomacy.[40] An important part of this appears to be the "authority of voice" that "stems from a knowledge practice primarily informed by material-centric disciplines . . . rooted in a discourse of scientific knowledge as apolitical, objective and value neutral."[41] This authority, exercised by the expert (and not the sponsor state) over a specific (and circumscribed) technical domain of materiality cannot be mistaken for bureaucratic or political decision-making, yet also allows a demonstration of both the capabilities and positive disposition of the sponsoring state.

Conclusion

As the concept of heritage diplomacy highlights the hitherto unnoticed positioning of preservation for international cooperation, peace-building, and geopolitical influence, it is timely that the role of the preservation expert, so structurally and symbolically central, is given attention. Away from proximity with the preservation object in the field, in the conference rooms of international preservation governance we see how that expertise comes to be shaped by its environment and by its expected function. Using the typologies of materiality and bureaucracy may be a useful lens to assess the symbolic role and value of expertise in these moments, and how it comes to inform the practices of heritage diplomacy.

Biography
Luke James is a PhD candidate at the Alfred Deakin Institute for Citizenship and Globalisation at Deakin University, Melbourne, Australia. His research investigates the role of technical expertise in the World Heritage system and global cultural governance. He has worked in international historic preservation for the Australian Government and with UNESCO and was formerly a heritage, planning, and environment lawyer. He has been published in the *International Journal of Cultural Policy* and the Australia ICOMOS journal *Historic Environment,* and he has guest lectured at Deakin University and Brandenburg University of Technology, Cottbüs, Germany.

Notes
I am very grateful to Professor Tim Winter for organizing the panel at the Association of Critical Heritage Studies conference, Canberra, 2014, at which an early version of this paper was presented.
[1] Christina Marie Luke and Morag M. Kersel, *U.S. Cultural Diplomacy and Archaeology: Soft Power, Hard Heritage* (New York: Routledge, 2012).

2 Chinese Academy of Cultural Heritage, *Angkor Wat Project,* http://english.cach
.org.cn/col/col1582/index.html.

3 Christoph Brumann, "Multilateral Ethnography: Entering the World Heritage
Arena," *Max Plank Institute for Social Anthropology Working Papers* (Halle, Germany: Max Planck Institute for Social Anthropology, 2012), http://www.eth.mpg
.de/cms/en/publications/working_papers/pdf/mpi-eth-working-paper-0136
.pdf; Lynn Meskell, "Transacting UNESCO World Heritage: Gifts and Exchanges on
a Global Scale," *Social Anthropology* 23, no. 1 (2015): 3-21; Tim Winter, "Heritage
Diplomacy and Australia's Responses to a Shifting Landscape of International
Conservation," *Alfred Deakin Research Institute Working Paper* no. 45 (2014),
http://www.deakin.edu.au/research-services/forms/v/7899/wps-45w.pdf; Tim
Winter, "Heritage Diplomacy," *International Journal of Heritage Studies* (2015):
1–19.

4 Tim Winter, "Heritage Conservation Futures in An Age of Shifting Global Power,"
Journal of Social Archaeology (2014): 1-21.

5 Tim Winter, "'Just Wear More Jewellery Darling, Big Rings, Up the Arm, the Heavier
the Better': Heritage Diplomacy and the Crafting of International Conservation
Policy," *Deakin University Cultural Heritage Centre for the Asia Pacific Presentation,*
Melbourne, September 24, 2014.

6 Salvador Muñoz Viñas, *Contemporary Theory of Conservation* (Oxford: Elsevier
Butterworth-Heinemann, 2005), 10–12, quoted in Tim Winter "Beyond Eurocentrism? Heritage Conservation and the Politics of Difference," *International Journal
of Heritage Studies* 20, no. 2 (2014): 9.

7 Denis Byrne, *Counterheritage: Critical Perspectives on Heritage Conservation in
Asia* (Abingdon, Oxon: Routledge, 2014), 22.

8 Tim Winter, "Clarifying the Critical in Critical Heritage Studies," *International Journal of Heritage Studies* 19 no. 6 (2013): 533.

9 Ibid. It is significant to note in this context that within the list of challenges cited
by Winter we find staple subjects of mainstream diplomatic practice today and, not
surprisingly, issues that arise in various forms as subjects of heritage diplomacy.

10 Max Weber, "Bureaucracy," in *Classical Sociological Theory*, ed. Craig J. Calhoun,
Joseph Gerteis, James W. Moody, Steven Pfaff, and Indermohan Virk, 328-38
(Chichester, West Sussex; Malden, MA: John Wiley & Sons, 2012).

11 The International Council on Monuments and Sites.

12 United Nations Educational, Scientific and Cultural Organization, "World Heritage
Committee — Decision — 39COM 8B.14 — Sites of Japan's Meiji Industrial Revolution:
Iron and Steel, Shipbuilding and Coal Mining, Japan," http://whc.unesco.org/en
/decisions/6364.

13 *International Charter for the Conservation and Restoration of Monuments and
Sites (The Venice Charter 1964),* http://www.icomos.org/charters/venice_e.pdf.

14 Dominic Walker, "Local World Heritage: Relocating Expertise in World Heritage
Management," in *Who Needs Experts? Counter-mapping Cultural Heritage,* ed.
John Schofield, 181-201 (Farnham, UK: Ashgate, 2014); Luke James and Tim Winter,
"Expertise and the Making of World Heritage Policy," *International Journal of
Cultural Policy* (2015): 1-16; Lucas Lixinski, "International Cultural Heritage Regimes,
International Law, and the Politics of Expertise," *International Journal of Cultural
Property* 20, no. 4 (2013): 407-29.

15 Dominic Walker, "Local World Heritage," 185.

16 Lucas Lixinski, "International Cultural Heritage Regimes," 411.

17 Ibid.

18 Tim Winter, "Heritage Tourism: The Dawn of a New Era?" in *Heritage and Globalization,* ed. Colin Long and Sophia Labadi (Abingdon, Oxon; New York: Routledge,
2010), 188–89.

19 United Nations Educational, Scientific, and Cultural Organization, "Sites of
Japan's Meiji Industrial Revolution."

20 James and Winter, "Expertise and the Making of World Heritage Policy."

21 Ibid., 7.

22 David Mosse, "Politics and Ethics: Ethnographies of Expert Knowledge and Professional Identities," in *Policy Worlds: Anthropology and the Analysis of Contemporary Power,* ed. Cris Shore, Susan Wright and Davide Però (New York: Berghahn
Books, 2011), 50-67.

23 Ibid., 56.

24 Ibid., 62.

25 See, for example, Bruno Latour, *Science in Action: How to Follow Scientists and
Engineers through Society* (Cambridge, Mass.: Harvard University Press, 1987); John
Law, *Organizing Modernity* (Oxford, UK: Blackwell, 1994). See also, Harry M. Collins
and Robert Evans, *Rethinking Expertise* (Chicago: University of Chicago Press, 2007).

26 United Nations Educational, Scientific and Cultural Organization (UNESCO), *Convention Concerning the Protection of the World Cultural and Natural Heritage* (Paris:

United Nations Educational, Scientific and Cultural Organization, 1972), http://whc
.unesco.org/archive/convention-en.pdf, Preamble.

27 UNESCO, *Operational Guidelines for the Implementation of the World Heritage
Convention,* Articles 77–119 (Paris: United Nations Educational, Scientific and
Cultural Organization, 2015), http://whc.unesco.org/document/137843.

28 The International Council on Monuments and Sites.

29 The International Union for the Conservation of Nature.

30 The International Centre for the Study of the Preservation and Restoration of
Cultural Property.

31 UNESCO, *Convention Concerning the Protection of the World Cultural and Natural
Heritage,* Articles 9(3); 8(3).

32 Lynn Meskell, "The Rush to Inscribe: Reflections on the 35th Session of the World
Heritage Committee, UNESCO Paris, 2011," *Journal of Field Archaeology* 37, no. 2
(2012): 145–51; Lynn Meskell, Claudia Liuzza, Enrico Bertacchini, and Donatella
Saccone, "Multilateralism and UNESCO World Heritage: Decision-Making, States
Parties, and Political Processes," *International Journal of Heritage Studies* (2014):
1–18; Enrico Bertacchini, Claudia Liuzza, and Lynn Meskell, "Shifting the Balance
of Power in the UNESCO World Heritage Committee: An Empirical Assessment,"
International Journal of Cultural Policy (2015): 1–21.

33 Bertacchini, Liuzza, and Meskell, "Shifting the Balance of Power," 16.

34 Brazil, Russia, India, China. Lynn Meskell, Claudia Liuzza, Enrico Bertacchini, and
Donatella Saccone, "Multilateralism and UNESCO World Heritage," 10.

35 Bertacchini, Liuzza, and Meskell, "Shifting the Balance of Power," 6.

36 International Council on Monuments and Sites, *2015 Evaluations of Nominations
of Cultural and Mixed Properties to the World Heritage List* (Charenton-le-Pont,
France: Secrétariat ICOMOS International, 2015), 271.

37 International Council on Monuments and Sites, *2014 Evaluations of Nominations
of Cultural and Mixed Properties to the World Heritage List* (Paris, France: Secrétariat
ICOMOS International, 2014), 77.

38 International Council on Monuments and Sites, *2015 Evaluations of Nominations,*
72.

39 Tim Winter, "Heritage Diplomacy and Australia's Responses to a Shifting Landscape of International Conservation."

40 Jessica C. E. Gienow-Hecht and Mark C. Donfried, eds., "Introduction" to *Searching for a Cultural Diplomacy,* 4–9 (New York: Berghahn Books, 2010).

41 Tim Winter, "Clarifying the Critical in Critical Heritage Studies," 539.

1. New Delhi, U.S. Embassy. Edward Durell Stone, 1954–59. Photograph courtesy U.S. Department of State.

Jane C. Loeffler

The State Department and the Politics of Preservation
Why Few U.S. Embassies Are Landmarks

It is just possible that the U.S. State Department really doesn't want to know its history. This curious observation occurs to me after decades of piecing together the unexplored past associated with the most tangible evidence of America's overseas diplomatic presence: its embassies. Those buildings cannot speak for themselves, but when documented they tell a remarkable story of political and cultural aspiration and diplomatic accomplishment set amidst an ever changing and challenging landscape.

One would think that knowing as much as possible about these buildings would be a priority for the department that buys, builds, and maintains properties overseas. One would think so particularly when spokesmen for the department publicly state that caring for properties that are recognized as historically significant furthers its diplomatic agenda. But this is not necessarily so.

It certainly was not so back in the 1950s and '60s when records pertaining to embassies were periodically "destroyed and thrown out," according to William McCullough, assistant director for building and design at the State Department's Office of Foreign Buildings Operations (FBO).[1] Interviewed in 1992, McCullough described how "nobody paid attention" when things regularly disappeared. One administrative officer, he said, packed up old deeds to historic properties and other papers, possibly documents pertaining to Jefferson's tenure as ambassador, and simply took them with him when he left FBO.

This was certainly peculiar as records management procedure, but not unusual for an office routinely ignoring the mandate to send its official records to the National Archives for processing and storage. FBO preferred instead to stash one-of-a-kind archives in desk drawers or what was ominously described to this researcher as "off-site." The failure to convey records to NARA is the main reason researchers, including many scholars from overseas, can find so little about the acquisition, design, and construction of U.S. diplomatic buildings among State Department archives at College Park.

Linking Modern Architecture to Public Diplomacy
William Slayton took the helm of FBO in 1978. What was unusual about Slayton, according to McCullough, was that he was "one director who desperately wanted to have a history written."[2]

Future Anterior
Volume XIII, Number 1
Summer 2016

To that end, his interests coincided with those of Bates Lowry, director of the National Building Museum, who proposed an opening exhibition on U.S. embassy architecture as a way of launching Washington's first and only museum dedicated to buildings.

In 1980, Slayton agreed to collaborate with Lowry on an exhibition. As Lowry's sole curator, I huddled with him in a corner of the still unrestored Pension Building trying to imagine how to gather information on buildings neither of us could identify. He assured me that nothing had been written on the subject. He was right.

Slayton came to FBO from the American Institute of Architects, the professional organization of U.S. architects. Although not an architect himself, he was eager to celebrate the contributions private architects had made to the State Department's architectural legacy. Lowry hoped to present mid-century modern masterpieces, such as Edward Durell Stone's popularly acclaimed landmark in New Delhi or Eero Saarinen's more hotly debated one in London; Slayton hoped to include embassy work in progress by architects he had commissioned, including Frederic Bassetti, Frank Gehry, George Hartman, Richard Meier, James Stewart Polshek, Ben Thompson, and Harry Wolf.[3]

At FBO back in 1980, librarian/archivist Lore Mika presided over a note card collection, hand-written job lists, boxed slide files, and a wondrous Lectriever, jam-packed with everything from snapshots of plumbing to professional photographs of finished projects by architects from Gropius and Breuer to those with no names at all. While perusing her records, I learned from Ms. Mika that she was the wife of a U.S. Foreign Service officer posted to Ouagadougou. Working with her was the beginning of my education in the geography of the State Department.

But I quickly found that information on those lists and cards was incomplete and not accurate enough to be used as the basis for an exhibition. The files comingled projects that were built with those that were never built. John Carl Warnecke's embassy project in Bangkok and Charles Goodman's in Reykjavik, two that were never built, were listed among those that were.[4] And incorrect architects were linked to some projects—Mies van de Rohe was listed for Mexico City on one list when that commission went to Southwestern Architects, and Goodman's name was paired with Lima, when the architects for that project were Keyes & Lethbridge.[5] It was also almost impossible to distinguish among projects for which programs had changed, as occurred in Tangier where architect Hugh Stubbins designed two totally different projects, years apart.

For a variety of reasons, including a lack of funds and bad timing, possibly the result of the 444-day hostage crisis centered on the U.S. Embassy in Tehran, the museum canceled its plans for the exhibition. There was, however, an unexpected windfall. On leaving the museum, I eventually returned to graduate school, wrote a doctoral dissertation based on a paper I published in the *Journal of the Society of Architectural Historians* (1990), and expanded that dissertation into a book, *The Architecture of Diplomacy: Building America's Embassies* (1998).

So Slayton got a history after all — if that was what he really wanted. Those who knew him professionally thought he was maybe more interested in furthering the interests of star architects with high-profile commissions abroad than he was in calling attention to the design dimension of public diplomacy. The several FBO directors who followed him were Foreign Service officers who were less expansive and more practical minded. All were open with historical records, but what they had to share was limited. Even the minutes of the celebrated architectural review panel, among the most valuable of the historical records stored at FBO, were incomplete on their own.[6]

State Historians Do Not Chronicle Buildings

For a more complete picture of State Department operations, I turned to its Historian's Office, assuming that an office, staffed by historians, would share my enthusiasm for fact. It did, but there was a caveat — what the Office of the Historian focuses on is the publication of the official documentary record of U.S. foreign relations, and compiling and publishing those records is such a cosmic endeavor that there is no apparent time or money for foreign relations involving buildings. Dr. William Z. Slany was historian of the Department of State when I was most involved in my research; it was he who told me that building history was simply beyond the purview of what his office could handle. But instead of suggesting that my project was unimportant, he enthusiastically approved it and directed his staff historians to assist me however they could. In the days before the Internet, that help was crucial. I could not have pieced together the history without the copies of internal (not classified!) State/FBO correspondence they shared or the ongoing fact-checking support he and his staff provided.[7]

It is worth noting, however, that within the State Department the Historian's Office operates within the Bureau of Public Affairs, reporting to the under secretary for Public Diplomacy and Public Affairs, who reports directly to the secretary of state. By contrast, FBO reports to the under secretary for Management, a different division entirely. Thus Dr. Slany had no connection whatsoever to FBO. Neither he nor his successors were in any position to recommend archival improvements there — or anything else, for that matter. How FBO kept its records (or did not) was its own business.

Cohen Introduces Heritage Mandate

For FBO to change its own relationship to history, change had to come from within the management sphere itself, and that is precisely what happened. Under Secretary for Management Bonnie Cohen came to State in 1997 from the Interior Department, where she served as assistant secretary for Policy, Management, and Budget. Before that, she had been at the National Trust for Historic Preservation, where she had honed a strong interest in history and preservation. At State, Cohen found herself responsible not only for FBO but also for the Foreign Service Institute and bureaus related to diplomatic security, administration, human resources, the State Department's diplomatic reception rooms, foreign missions in D.C., and more. She reported directly to Secretary of State Madeleine Albright.

It was Under Secretary Cohen who led the drive that first made "preservation" a respectable word at the State Department, if not a totally workable or trusted policy priority, and it was she who facilitated the creation of the *Secretary's Register of Culturally Significant Property,* an ambitious effort launched in 2000 to publicize diplomatic holdings of exceptional importance and spotlight the Department's rich and largely unrecognized architectural and cultural history.

Among Cohen's early moves as under secretary was her implementation of a new policy aimed at bringing foreign buildings into alignment with President Bill Clinton's 1996 Executive Order on Federal Buildings in the United States, an order that directed the government to locate domestic federal facilities in older buildings in downtown areas to stimulate growth in those areas and save historic structures.[8] She directed FBO to do much the same thing with foreign buildings—to utilize and maintain, where possible, "historic properties and districts, especially those located in central business areas," and to do so in accordance with "guidelines established in 1990 by the Secretary of the Interior's Standards for Historic Preservation Projects," as long as those guidelines did not conflict with preservation guidelines of the host nation.

On March 16, 1998, Cohen wrote to Richard Moe, president of the National Trust for Historic Preservation, citing the new policy as an "important step linking the domestic building policy of the United States with our operations overseas." She explained, "We have, with the help of the Trust . . . done our best to take account of preservation as we, the country's owner and operator of buildings overseas, do the United States' business."[9] Deputy Assistant Secretary Patsy Thomasson signed the directive on behalf of FBO.[10] But just five months later, in August, terrorists attacked U.S. embassies in Nairobi and Dar es Salaam killing 224 people and injuring more than

SECRETARY'S REGISTER OF CULTURALLY SIGNIFICANT PROPERTY (in order listed):

Tangier, (former) legation, Morocco (2001)
Prague, *Schoenborn Palace,* chancery, Czech Republic (2001)
Tokyo, ambassador's residence, Japan (2001)
Seoul, legation, embassy guest house, South Korea (2001)
Rome, *Palazzo Margherita & Twin Villas,* chancery, Italy (2001)
Paris, *Hôtel Talleyrand,* chancery annex, Paris, France (2001)
London, *Winfield House,* ambassador's residence, England (2001)
Buenos Aires, *Palacio Bosch,* ambassador's residence, Argentina (2002)
Tirana, chancery and former residence, Albania (2004)
New Delhi, embassy compound, India (2004)
Hanoi, ambassador's residence, Vietnam (2004)
Oslo, *Villa Otium,* ambassador's residence, Norway (2004)
Alexandria, American Center, Egypt (2006)
Madrid, *Byne House,* DCM residence, Spain (2006)
Manila, chancery, The Philippines (2006)
Athens, chancery, Greece (2006)
Brussels, *Truman Hall* (NATO), Belgium (2006)
Rome, *Villa Taverna,* ambassador's residence, Italy (2008)
Prague, *Villa Petschek,* ambassador's residence, Czech Republic (2008)
Paris, *Hôtel Rothschild,* ambassador's residence, France (2008)
Baguio, ambassador's residence, The Philippines (2012)
Florence, *Palazzo Canevaro,* consulate, Italy (2012)
Moscow, *Spaso House,* ambassador's residence, Russia (2012)
Tripoli, The American Cemetery, Libya (2012)
Washington, D.C., *Blair House,* diplomatic guest house, United States (2012)
Casablanca, *Villa Mirador,* consulate general's residence, Morocco (2014)

2. Secretary's Register of Culturally Significant Property, 2014.

4,000; the optimistic idea of locating new U.S. embassies in densely built-up historic downtown districts quickly faded as a planning option.

This was probably the first time, however, that anyone proposed applying Interior guidelines to State properties (aside, perhaps, from the aberrant listing of the old Tangier Legation on the National Register of Historic Places). And it was the first time that FBO officially recognized "preservation" as a planning priority. Until that time, no one at FBO had dared to utter that very charged word.

After all, many at FBO erroneously equated preservation with protection and/or permanence, neither of which were deemed well suited to diplomatic facilities that needed to respond to changes in foreign policy and be able to adapt to a rapidly changing political landscape. There may have been pride in having the Tangier Legation listed on the National Register and also designated a National Historic Landmark, but few at State wanted constraints on their properties imposed

by Interior, a Cabinet-level agency with a different outlook and
agenda.

Architects List State's Historic Properties

There were individuals, however, who championed creating
some sort of comparable list as a way to recognize the large
number of historically significant properties owned and leased
by the State Department. Chief architect Patrick Collins was
perhaps the most ardent supporter of this idea within FBO.
With the addition of preservation architect Kevin Lee Sarring
to his staff and support from those at FBO concerned with art
and furnishings, Collins was able to push his idea forward with
Cohen as under secretary.

First, Collins created an ad hoc committee of cultural resource professionals within FBO. Sarring, assisted by architect
Robert Parke, began by identifying ninety-five key properties
using modified preservation criteria such as those in use at
Interior. By July 1998, FBO had expanded that collection into
an inventory of some 155 properties identified as architecturally, culturally, or historically significant.[11]

Not only did that initial list include shared cultural assets
such as the Palazzo Corpi in Istanbul, one of America's first embassies when purchased in 1907, and Spaso House in Moscow
or the former Rothschild mansion in Paris, both purchased
for use as ambassador's residences, but it also included
landmarks that gave American diplomacy high visibility at the
height of the Cold War when the State Department commissioned prominent modernists to design new embassies in
Accra, Athens, Baghdad, Dublin, Karachi, London, New Delhi,
The Hague, and other world capitals.

That first list of 155 properties was not exhaustive, but it
was broadly inclusive—listing some buildings that had been
already sold or abandoned, such as Harry Weese's in Accra
(the U.S. Embassy had moved out in 1983)—underscoring its
intended value as a historical resource.[12] This is a key point,
because later Departmental efforts clearly sought to downplay
the scope of the original intent.

When published in August 1998, *The Architecture of
Diplomacy* included chronological lists of State Department
properties, dates, names of architects, and history—most previously unexamined. Under Secretary Cohen greeted the book
with enthusiasm and hosted a State Department event in its
honor. Based on that work, she asked me to submit a proposal
that could be used as a prototype for an inventory of what she
called "heritage properties."

Early in 1999, I submitted a proposal to her identifying
sixteen properties that played a significant role in U.S. history

3. Accra, former U.S. Embassy. Harry Weese (1956–59). Embassy decommissioned in 1983 and photographed here in 2001. Photograph copyright E. Gill Lui, 2001.

as a result of architectural and/or diplomatic distinction or because of local distinction of some other sort.[13] Thinking that a representative sample would be best, I selected properties that represented each of State's geographic bureaus and also each of the major types of buildings for which FBO was responsible: residences and office buildings; purchased/leased and purpose-built; and historic landmarks with local significance versus those with specific ties to themes of U.S. (e.g., the Barbary Wars) or world history (e.g. mid-century modern architecture). I did this unaware of parallel efforts ongoing at FBO. The sixteen examples included: Havana ER; Helsinki EOB; Istanbul COB *Palazzo Corpi*; London EOB; Moscow ER *Spaso House*; New Delhi EOB compound; Rio de Janeiro COB; Paris EOBX *Hôtel Talleyrand*; Paris ER *Hôtel Pontalba*; Prague EOB *Schoenborn Palace*; Prague ER *Petchek Palace*; Riga EOB; Shanghai COB; Tangier LEG; Tokyo DCMR; Tokyo ER.[14]

I learned of FBO's similar involvement in documentation efforts when I was invited to collaborate on another proposal concerning mid-century modern buildings commissioned by FBO at the heyday of its postwar building program.[15] The original title on that proposal was: "U.S. Embassies Built by the State Department in New Delhi, Karachi, Baghdad, Accra, London, The Hague, Athens, and Dublin between 1954 and 1964."[16] It ended up shortened to "Embassies of the Cold War:

4. Athens, U.S. Embassy. Walter Gropius/TAC (1956–61). Building currently being rehabilitated. Functions have been moved to adjacent high-security annex. Photograph courtesy U.S. Department of State.

Incubators of Contextual Modernism" when FBO submitted it for a Millennium Award honoring eight great American modernists, five of whom were also AIA Gold Medal winners.[17]

Albright Launches Expansive *Register* in 2000

By late in 2000, the various proposals, together with material culled from the extensive inventory FBO had already prepared, combined to form the *Secretary of State's Register of Culturally Significant Property*. Records, including an "Action Memorandum" from Under Secretary Cohen to Secretary Albright, make it clear that the Register was never intended as a honorary list of a few notable properties, but was intended as nothing less than "an official list of overseas property, architecture and other significant objects important to the diplomatic history of the United States."[18]

In her memorandum, Cohen explained that the Register was meant to be analogous to the *National Register of Historic Places* maintained by the Secretary of the Interior, and she also explicitly stated that Registry status would in no way interfere with the Department's ability to alter or sell property. Moreover, she said, Registry status had the potential to boost property value. She cited the Office of Foreign Buildings Operations as the entity charged with implementing policies connected to the Register and its Cultural Resources Committee as the planning group that would determine inclusion based on these criteria:

1. Designation or acknowledgment by a government as a
   significant property
2. Part of the United States' overseas heritage
3. Association with a significant historical event of person
4. Important architecture and/or by an important architect
5. Distinctive theme or assembly
6. Unique object or visual feature
7. Archeological site

Further, Cohen asked Secretary Albright to approve developing background information on selected properties as a way of launching the project and reaching out to the diplomatic community and the larger general public, and invited the Secretary to host an inaugural ceremony.[19]

Just before leaving office, on January 4, 2001, Albright announced the Register at a ceremony held appropriately in the Diplomatic Reception Rooms at Main State. Standing among easels featuring posters showing seven prototype properties, she made it clear that the Register highlighted the value of more than 150 similar properties. She declared the Register a means of providing all such properties with "greater visibility and protection as landmarks" and explained that the new roster in its entirety was "part of President Clinton's millennial effort to save America's cultural treasures and history and promote the nation's arts and humanities."[20]

The selected properties included six shared cultural assets, purchased or received as gifts by the USG for diplomatic use, and one overseas American landmark, the ambassador's residence in Tokyo, among the earliest projects built after Congress funded site acquisition and embassy construction for the first time as part of a program to improve U.S. representation abroad. The seven shared assets included: **Tangier** Old Legation (acquired 1821); **Prague** EOB *Schoenborn Palace* (purchased 1925); **Tokyo** ER (Raymond & Magonigle, 1926–31, built by USG); **Seoul** Old Legation/Guest House (purchased 1888); **Rome** EOB *Palazzo Margherita & Twin Villas* (purchased 1946 & 1931); **Paris** EOBX *Hôtel Talleyrand* (purchased 1950); and **London** ER *Winfield House* (acquired 1946).

The optimism of that moment evaporated later that year in a series political upheavals and international explosions. What Secretary Albright aptly described as a chance to capture and share history was lost—at least then. The Register never expanded as hoped or expected, but grew only in piecemeal fashion for more than a decade, buffeted by political and personal whims. One such decision was to eliminate from consideration any property that had been sold or might be sold. That effectively erased those properties from historical memory.

5. Karachi, former U.S. Consulate General, which had been the Embassy until 1960, when Pakistan's capital moved to Islamabad. Neutra & Alexander (1955–59). This building was decommissioned in 2011. Photograph courtesy U.S. Department of State.

Some already lost in that fashion include the former U.S. Embassy in Ottawa (1928–32), a neoclassical palazzo designed by noted American architect Cass Gilbert just before he designed the U.S. Supreme Court in Washington, D.C., his last major work. Other embassies similarly lost include those in Karachi, Baghdad, Accra, London, and The Hague—five of the eight identified by FBO in its 1999 millennium proposal as key landmarks of the Cold War era.[21]

OBO Narrows Register's Focus

What happened in 2001 that led to such a change in direction? After becoming secretary of state, Colin Powell reorganized FBO, installing General Charles Williams (who earned his military title in the Army Corps of Engineers), as head of the foreign building program. Powell had Williams report directly to him, and FBO was renamed to reflect its new status as a bureau within the department. The Bureau of Overseas Buildings Operations (OBO) formally replaced FBO on May 15, 2001. Williams, who enjoyed a panoramic view of the Kennedy Center and Main State beyond from his penthouse offices in Rosslyn, Virginia, preferred to manage a compartmentalized bureaucracy in which the individual parts could communicate only through him. He installed himself as chief operating officer and sent a clear message to subordinates to align themselves with his priorities. Openness was not among those priorities.

Responding to brutal terrorist attacks on diplomats, soldiers, and civilians in and near U.S. embassies in Beirut, Nairobi, Dar es Salaam, and at scores of other targets worldwide, the 1999 the Overseas Presence Advisory Panel (OPAP) had condemned the "shockingly shabby" conditions at many State Department facilities. That led Congress to enact the Secure Embassy Construction and Counterterrorism Act (SECCA), which codified security requirements, such as the 100-foot setback, for the first time. OBO faced challenges markedly different from those faced by its predecessor, FBO, even before those challenges multiplied again on September 11, 2001.

Pushed by Congress to come to terms with the security mandate that had been so difficult for FBO to confront, OBO transformed its building program in short order. To his credit, Williams oversaw the construction of more than fifty new embassies and consulates providing U.S. diplomats with sorely needed safe and modern workplaces. In so doing, however, he introduced a "standard embassy design" (SED), used design/build to give direct control to individual general contractors, and he allowed real estate professionals to make what were in fact diplomatic and strategic decisions about embassy location. He ultimately alienated diplomats, who condemned walled and inaccessible embassy enclaves that compromised the conduct of diplomacy.[22] He also alienated architects, who played only a limited role in the design/build process used to create those enclaves. He drew further ire from design professionals when he abandoned State's highly acclaimed architectural review panel in 2004, its fiftieth anniversary year.

Williams also seized upon the ambient fear to restrict access to records, photos, and people. Routine requests for photos of widely published embassy buildings for use even in lectures required his approval, and that approval was often denied. If Williams was apprehensive about lending photos for academic use, he was certainly not keen on expanding a Register for popular dissemination. Only ten properties were added to the historical list, which was little touted during

6. Oslo, U.S. Ambassador's Residence, *Villa Otium* (detail over entrance). Jugendstil landmark designed by Henrik Bull in 1911, purchased by USG as U.S. Legation in 1924. Photograph by Robert Loeffler, 2011.

his tenure.[23] The ten he added were: Buenos Aires ER *Palacio Bosch* (purchased 1929); Hanoi ER (purchased 1995); New Delhi EOB (Edward Durell Stone, 1954–59, built by USG); Oslo ER, former LEG, *Villa Otium* (purchased 1924); Tirana EOB (Wyeth & Sullivan, 1929, built by USG); Alexandria American Center (purchased 1962); Athens EOB (TAC, Walter Gropius, 1956–61, built by USG); Brussels U.S. Mission to NATO *Truman Hall* (acquired 1904); Madrid DCMR *Byne House* (purchased 1944); and Manila EOB (Juan M. de Guzman, 1934).[24]

More than how many or few he added, Williams changed the list's fundamental purpose when he had it labeled "honorific" to assuage doubts about the selection process. That term appears in 2004 in a memo from Williams to Secretary Powell asking the secretary to approve adding properties in New Delhi, Tirana, Hanoi, and Oslo to the Register. In that memo, Williams included the phrase: "Registration is honorific and insures that necessary alterations preserve cultural value."[25] The term "honorific" appears in subsequent publications and is still used to describe the Register's purpose.

There is a big difference between a list that is intended as "an official list of overseas property, architecture and other significant objects important to the diplomatic history of the United States" and one that is merely honorific.[26] The U.S. Postal Service, for example, pays homage to great Americans by creating postage stamps in their honor, but USPS makes no pretense at trying to create stamps honoring all the Americans who have played important roles at making this country great. It has an *honorific* program. If the National Portrait Gallery collected only the portraits of those Americans who appeared on postage stamps, its collection would be little more than a skewed sample. We could never know our history from it—unless the point of such a history is quite different from what we, as historians, think it is. An honorific list is little more than a public relations gesture on behalf of those who compile it, awarding recognition for compliance or where there is opportunity for political gain, and denying it where there is no ostensible gain, The decision to list only currently owned property on the Register, for example, suggests that the State Department sees no reason to honor "lost" property, no matter how significant its role in American architectural, cultural, or diplomatic history. Certainly, this is a loss to historians who want to better understand our overseas presence, how it has evolved and how it is likely to change in the future. If we erase the past from our records, we can study only the present, and that is, indeed, a chilling thought.

Preservation Policy: More False Starts

Williams departed OBO in a scandal concerning the construction of the mega-embassy in Baghdad in 2007. Foreign Service officers Richard Shinnick and Adam Namm followed him as acting OBO directors and restored a sense of balance to the organization. It was under Shinnick's tenure as OBO director, *ad interim,* that Vivien Woofter was named to coordinate a newly created Cultural Heritage Branch (CHB) within OBO.

After a forty-year career with the federal government—at GSA, the White House, and more recently as head of FBO's interior design and furnishings division—Woofter became heritage preservation officer of the new office. In October 2008, with strong support from Under Secretary of State for Management Patrick Kennedy, Woofter organized an ambitious symposium, "Saving the Department's Treasures"—the first program to bring together curators, conservators, preservation officers, architects, engineers, housekeepers, and interior designers to address how to care for furniture, art, and artifacts owned by the State Department.[27]

In welcoming guests to the symposium, Under Secretary Kennedy cited the creation of the Cultural Heritage Branch as evidence that at last "our significant properties and collections will have a permanent champion."[28] With talks by experts from Winterthur and the Smithsonian, and presentations from others who shared experiences ranging from caring for antiques at England's Waddesdon Manor to maintaining masonry at Canterbury Cathedral, the symposium covered a wide range of conservation issues.

Regarding OBO cultural assets, director Shinnick declared that the CHB would prepare maintenance programs for all properties on the Secretary's Register and also for other assets within OBO's purview. In addition, he said, the CHB would determine eligibility for Register listing of additional properties. As Woofter explained it, the goal of OBO's new cultural management program was nothing less than to "develop a world class stewardship program dedicated to the proper conservation and maintenance of the Department's culturally significant properties and assets."[29]

But the excitement of that moment, like several other propitious moments before it, faded fast. OBO had added three properties to its Register in 2008, five in 2012, and one in 2014, but to outside observers the additions were beginning to seem increasingly curious and even far-fetched.

The new additions included: Paris ER *Hôtel Rothschild* (purchased 1948); Prague ER *Villa Petschek* (purchased 1948); Rome ER *Villa Taverna* (purchased 1948); Baguio ER (purchased 1938); Florence COB (purchased 1947), Moscow ER *Spaso House* (purchased 1934), Tripoli The American Cemetery (1804/2004), Washington, D.C., *Blair House* (purchased 1942), and Casablanca CGR *Villa Mirador* (purchased 1947).[30] While some were definitely distinguished, others seemed out of place on a list that omitted so many shoo-in landmarks. One such is the former Embassy in Ottawa. Another is the splendid *Palazzo Corpi* in Istanbul, the first USG-owned diplomatic facility in Europe, still owned by the State Department but currently leased to a Turkish developer for use as a luxury hotel and private club that also accommodates a public restaurant, a bar, and the Istanbul offices of the Hollings Center for International Dialogue.

Although it makes perfect sense for OBO to list purchased/gift properties on its Register as a way of showing respect for shared cultural heritage, it makes no sense to list such properties to the exclusion of those designed by U.S. architects and built by the State Department as part of a foreign building program that has largely defined America's overseas diplomatic presence since the early days of the Cold War. Out of the twenty-six properties on the Register, only five were built by the USG: 1) Tokyo ER and 2) Tirana ER/EOB — under

7. Istanbul, former U.S. Consulate General, *Palazzo Corpi*, now *Soho House*. Photograph copyright Caroline Mesrobian Hickman, 2015.

the auspices of the Foreign Services Buildings Commission; 3) New Delhi EOB and 4) Athens EOB — under the auspices of FBO; and 5) Manila EOB — under a special congressional appropriation. The remaining twenty-one were either acquired by gift or purchased. That suggests not only a preoccupation with acquired properties to the exclusion of those designed for the purpose of serving as diplomatic facilities, a particular challenge to American architects and engineers, but also a strong desire to use the Register as a means to win favor with host governments by citing shared assets, not as a means of documenting what is most "important to the diplomatic history of the United States."

Essentially, it is prioritizing public diplomacy over history, if the two need to be at odds. But they need not be at odds if the Register were to expand, for example, by adding most of the 140 historic properties built by the USG and identified *The Architecture of Diplomacy*. Columbia's Avery Architectural and Fine Arts Library acquired the research papers associated with that book in 2014.[31] OBO has yet to investigate that research collection, but the fact that OBO often finds itself searching for items, from missing pages of minutes about the original design for New Delhi to an entirely missing 1987 feasibility study for the Tokyo DCMR, does suggest that its own historical resources are incomplete. Expanding the Register and the materials that

8. Istanbul, former U.S. Consulate General, *Palazzo Corpi,* now *Soho House*. Photograph copyright Caroline Mesrobian Hickman, 2015.

support it is one way to enhance our understanding of history, to develop what Woofter earlier described as "a world class stewardship program."

Woofter herself resurfaced in 2013 with the title "Heritage Conservation Advisor" and a new cause called the *Fund to Conserve,* a public/private partnership with the goal of raising funds to restore and maintain cultural property at embassies abroad. In its inaugural pamphlet, the Fund showed photos of old and new buildings, including the former Legation in Tangier (acquired 1821) and the new Embassy in Ottawa (1999), along with paintings, artifacts, and antiques. The little publication, also available online, raised more questions than it answered. Its definitions were vague, its agenda was unclear, and it was impossible to tell how this Fund differed from others ostensibly dedicated to similar purposes. Thinking, mistakenly, it seems, that the publication could use close editing, I submitted a list of questions/suggestions to OBO's director at that time. My queries included these:

1. How are you defining preservation versus conservation?
2. How expansive is your definition of "culturally signifi-cant property"? Do you include art, furniture, furnish-ings, and also buildings and gardens? What about personal papers, photographs, maps, souvenirs, flags, representation of eagles, official seals, clothing,

9. Ottawa, former U.S. Embassy, previously the American Legation. Cass Gilbert (1928–32). When the U.S. Embassy moved to a new facility nearby in 1999, this building was transferred to the government of Canada. Although it was supposed to become the Portrait Gallery of Canada, that has never occurred. But the government of Canada listed it on the Canadian Register in 2010 citing heritage character derived from its architecture, its history (both American and Canadian associations), and its environmental significance. Photograph courtesy U.S. Department of State.

artifacts—more or less? Explain. This affects potential donations.

3. From your *Fund to Conserve* booklet, it is impossible to know what the Fund hopes to accomplish, who heads it, and how it differs from other groups. How does it differ from *Foundation for Art and Preservation in Embassies* (FAPE), for example? How does it connect to your *Art in Embassies Program*? Or to the *U.S. Diplomacy Center,* State's new museum of diplomacy that will have its own collection of artifacts and culturally significant diplomatic objects?

4. Who at OBO is responsible for reports on historic structures; how are selections made for such studies?

5. Why doesn't the Register include properties that have been sold or could be sold? Many are among the most important in terms of our architectural and diplomatic history.

6. Could OBO add historians as professional advisors, such as the architects and industry representatives included on the IAP? State's Historian's Office also has an advisory panel, but those historians do not know architecture. With more than 3,500 properties worldwide, there is plenty of history within OBO's purview. Would this not be a good idea?

State Names New Heritage "Champion"

After two years of waiting, when it seemed evident that no one at OBO wanted to answer my questions, or no one *could* answer them, a piece of mildly encouraging news emerged—once again the State Department was reorganizing its heritage mandate, creating a newly constituted Office of Cultural Heritage within OBO, and seeking a director for that office. Soon after, Tobin Tracey, AIA, a professional preservation architect, was named to fill the slot. Tracey came to OBO from the National Park Service, where since 2004 he had been responsible for the maintenance and preservation of the historic portion of the White House. A graduate of Iowa State University, with a master of arts in historic preservation from Goucher, he headed a private architectural practice based in New England for twenty years before joining the Park Service.

If I had to explain this move, I'd say that Under Secretary Kennedy decided it was time, finally, to ensure that cultural heritage does have a "permanent champion."[32] Even back in 2008, it was evident that Woofter, though indefatigable and politically savvy, could not direct such an effort by herself. Given OBO's deeply vested interests, the advantages of bringing in outside expertise, and the necessity for up-to-date professional know-how, Tracey is a good choice for an agency once again on the verge of contemplating its history. The question is whether he will be allowed to do what he says he wants to do and deems necessary?

In an interview last November, Tracey acknowledged that he was just learning the ropes at OBO, and expressed cautious optimism about the task ahead. As he sees it, his first two challenges involve documentation: to identify culturally significant properties and to prepare what he calls "cultural significance studies" for them.[33] Together with his staff, he has already identified 130 "significant" properties from those owned or held by the State Department on long-term leases. (This compilation is most likely an updated version of the 2000 inventory—mainly the 155 properties minus those sold since that time or likely to be sold.) Using criteria drawn from Interior Department definitions, Tracey proposes to study the 130 properties to determine individual significance, to recommend additions to the existing Register, and to determine "preservation zones" to guide future improvements. The studies will form the basis for a stewardship program embracing all tangible diplomatic assets abroad, including art, antiques, furniture, landscapes, artifacts, and buildings.

"Exploring ways to make cultural assets more open to the public," Tracey says, is his third challenge. Eager to find new ways to gather and disseminate history, he is already imagining how he might share it via embassy open houses, virtual

10. London, U.S. Embassy. Eero Saarinen (1956–60). Trimmed in gold-colored anodized aluminum with a thirty-five-foot wide eagle on top overlooking Grosvenor Square. Photograph copyright Balthazar Korab, 1960, from Library of Congress, Balthazar Korab Archive.

tours, website resources, books, or using other media. As to gathering it, he has begun talks with Oxford University and with Iowa State University about a joint project involving Iowa's new historic preservation program, and other such projects could follow.

What Tracey cannot really discuss is the matter of transparency—one of the biggest challenges he confronts—because if his effort is to succeed as he envisions it, it needs to be open and collaborative. It needs to involve critical thinking on the multiple meanings attached to the terms *cultural asset, preservation, conservation,* and *significance,* and needs to better explain preservation to its various stakeholders as a planning strategy and not an end in itself. The secretive atmosphere that infuses so much discourse at OBO—not to be confused with a rightful concern for security—poses a real challenge to any administrator who strives to bring together information, people, and properties to expand knowledge and then to disseminate what is learned.

The risk of losing landmarks before they are documented is another major challenge. Structures in London, The Hague, and Oslo are among the many that are now being replaced. Tracey regrets that he lacks the resources to study such properties. Although each is undergoing a "decommissioning" process according to OBO protocols, that process is nothing he can more precisely explain. If it includes careful photographic documentation of architectural details, such as Saarinen's anodized aluminum "stars," for example, no one can say. This is where a little more transparency would be helpful—because

11. London, U.S. Embassy. Eero Saarinen (1956–60). Consular Section on first floor, with diagrid structural system above. Photograph copyright Balthazar Korab, 1960, from Library of Congress, Balthazar Korab Archive.

once an American-owned landmark such as London is lost, whether it is sold for demolition or reuse, it is gone. It may remain accessible as a structure, but in a new role elements are altered and the symbolic significance shifts. Thus meaning has time value that suffers from delay. With a conspicuous American eagle perched on its rooftop (an official symbol of USG presence that really should not have been construed as a permanent fixture by those who listed the building) and flanked at its base by statues of General Dwight Eisenhower and President Ronald Reagan, and with another statue of President Franklin Roosevelt and American war memorials in the park, Grosvenor Square is still a place steeped in American heritage and meriting recognition as such. Fully documenting the Saarinen building as the last marker of a U.S. diplomatic presence dating to 1785 would be a step in that direction — perhaps on a new *Secretary's List of Lost Landmarks*?

Why Reject History?

Maybe the London experience provides one clue as to why State has exhibited such a reluctance to know its past? In 2009, the City of Westminster granted the U.S. Embassy Grade II listed status as a protected local landmark.[34] Qatar's sovereign wealth fund purchased the chancery a month later for an estimated £500 million. According to published reports, the

12. The Hague, U.S. Embassy, featured on cover of "Building Diplomacy, The American Embassy in The Hague, Marcel Breuer, 1956–59," historic preservation report prepared in 2008 by Wijnand Galema et al., for The City of The Hague, which takes ownership of the Breuer building when the U.S. Embassy moves soon to a new suburban facility. Publication courtesy of The City of the Hague, Department of Urban Development (Rotterdam).

225,000 square foot building could be worth up to £1 billion when developed as a mixed-use project.[35] But if the Qataris had been able to demolish the landmark or alter its façade, could the sales price have gone higher? Maybe not, in a city that values the past. But maybe so—especially when that past was never much admired. And what if the buyer happens to have unlimited wealth and is readily spending it on London real estate? After all, Mayfair is already becoming London's most exclusive residential neighborhood. Encircled by some of the most expensive flats in the city, Grosvenor Square had one flat advertised at £18 million in 2014, and prices are expected to top £10,000 per square foot within a decade.[36]

If Embassy officials feared that "protecting" it as a historic structure would depress the Embassy's resale value, they might have hoped to avoid such a designation instead of welcoming it. They might even have looked askance at the historical sources that enabled such a listing.

Under Secretary Cohen predicted that a Register listing might boost property values, but it is possible, too, that others at State expect just the opposite and act intentionally or unintentionally to try to prevent prices from falling. Those who think they are thus protecting our assets see history as a foe. If we know too much about our overseas properties and maybe recognize them as important to our history, other nations will realize they are important, follow our example, and list them as significant locally — that might interfere with our ability to alter them or sell them at top dollar for redevelopment. Knowing little and saying nothing thus could be the best policy from the standpoint of real estate management. And it would also make sense as a way of keeping easy ammunition away from zealous preservationists or others who might want to go to bat on behalf of faraway landmarks that lack a ready constituency closer to home.

That is what happened, for example, in Karachi where Arif Belgaumi, a young Pakistani architect, tried unsuccessfully to rally the international community on behalf of the former U.S. Consulate, designed by Neutra & Alexander at the height of the Cold War. As Belgaumi pointed out in 2011,

> The decommissioning of the old US Consulate raised questions about the future of this modern masterpiece and perhaps presents opportunities for promoting US–Pakistan relations. The building is one of the few public buildings by Richard J. Neutra, an accomplished master of the late Modern Movement. As a fine example of the 1950s International Style, it is representative of the ferment and debate current at the time about the nature of architecture. The building is a part of world architectural heritage and particularly that of the United States and Pakistan. And as such must be preserved.[37]

The State Department is not in the business of saving actual buildings for posterity, nor should it be, but alarm over that prospect is enough, it seems, to dampen any enthusiasm for finding other ways of engaging in cultural diplomacy that embraces such assets. Over time, that reluctance, coupled with an ahistorical attitude, has evolved as a survival mechanism providing protection for those working in the real estate operation that is OBO. And it is probably the greatest threat to the heritage mandate.

This is no time to yearn for old-fashioned diplomacy, a nostalgic past, or buildings that are outdated and vulnerable. Documentation is the best way of capturing the diplomatic past and informing its future. The new Cultural Heritage Office can best meet the challenges ahead by focusing on ways to escape its insularity, making the most of its professional expertise, and connecting with other entities that collect and manage cultural assets both inside the State Department and beyond to strengthen its stewardship program. A good first step would be finding a link to the U.S. Diplomacy Center, the new museum within the State Department that aims to explore the past, present and future of U.S. diplomacy in order to see that our diplomatic buildings play a role in what is explored and presented there. And if as Tracey says, "Caring for distinguished historic properties in our portfolio furthers our diplomatic mission," then this could be just the right moment to embrace history broadly as a way of instilling confidence in that mission.

Biography
Jane C. Loeffler is a planner and architectural historian and author of *The Architecture of Diplomacy: Building America's Embassies* (1998, 2011), For her work, she received the Secretary's Open Forum Distinguished Public Service Award from the U.S. Department of State in 1998 and the Bureau of Overseas Buildings Operations Outstanding Recognition Award in 2010.

Dedicated to the memory of Russell V. Keune, whose recent loss deprives us of a pioneer in historic preservation.

Notes
[1] William McCullough, interview with author, May 18, 1992. The Jane C. Loeffler Collection of Research Papers on American Embassies, Avery Architectural and Fine Arts Library, Columbia University (Hereafter "Avery").
[2] Ibid. Although McCullough claimed that Paul Serey was asked to write a history, I don't think he actually wrote one. Rather, he seems to have repurposed an internal history that had been compiled earlier by OH/PA, ending around 1958–60. I received a copy of that document from Serey himself and another from OH/PA. It is available in Avery, under the title: "Inauguration of the Foreign Service Buildings Program."
[3] Jane C. Loeffler, *The Architecture of Diplomacy: Building America's Embassies* (New York: Princeton Architectural Press, 2011), 238.
[4] FBO historical document labeled "Early List from FBO." Avery.
[5] FBO historical document titled "Embassy Buildings," hand-dated circa 1960–61. Avery.
[6] Minutes of the FBO Architectural Advisory Committee (also known as the Panel and Board and briefly as Consultants), for the period January 21, 1954 – February 12, 1981. Avery.
[7] William Z. Slany, Official State Department endorsement letters, July 12, 1990 and January 24, 1996, Avery.
[8] Executive Order No. 13006, "Locating Federal Facilities on Historic Properties in Our Nation's Cities" (May 21, 1996), Fed. Reg. 61/102 (May 24, 1996), 26071, Avery.
[9] Bonnie R. Cohen to Richard Moe, March 16, 1998. Avery.
[10] A/FBO Policy and Procedures Directive No. RE005 (March 3, 1998), *Acquisition and Preservation of Historically, Architecturally, or Culturally Significant Property Overseas.* Avery.
[11] "Culturally Significant Properties Inventory (Draft)" and labeled "A/FBO/AP/RE/RPM-Ellen Enriquez," dated June 29, 1998, 16 pgs. Avery.

[12] Not every historically significant building was included on the 1998 draft listing of *Culturally Significant Properties Inventory*. The most notable omission of those buildings built by the USG was the U.S. Embassy, Ottawa, designed by Cass Gilbert in 1928. The most notable omission of those purchased by the USG was the Tokyo residence for the deputy chief of mission (DCMR), ascribed to several architects, but attributed to celebrated modernist Antonin Raymond by Sibley Jennings in his 1987 feasibility study of renovations to that structure. It appears that Jennings was retained to prepare that study by the U.S. Embassy in Tokyo, not by FBO in Washington, although an FBO representative assisted him. For further information, see J. L. Sibley Jennings, AIA, & Associates, Architects, *Feasibility Study, Proposed Remodeling of Architectural, Mechanical, Electrical, and Plumbing Systems for the Residence of the Deputy Chief of Mission (Property Number X04006), Tokyo, Japan, 1987* in Avery. A Raymond building would certainly have belonged in any inventory of architecturally important structures had it been recognized by FBO at the time.

[13] Loeffler to Bonnie R. Cohen, "Heritage Property Proposal as Millennium 2000 Project," (February 11, 1999), Avery.

[14] Abbreviations used: EOB = embassy office building (chancery); EOBX = embassy office building annex; COB = consular office building (consulate); ER = embassy residence or ambassador's residence; DCMR = deputy chief of mission residence; LEG = former legation property.

[15] Loeffler, "The Architecture of Diplomacy: Heyday of the U. S. Embassy-Building Program, 1954–1960," *Journal of the Society of Architectural Historians*, September 1990: 251–78.

[16] Loeffler with FBO, "Embassies of the Cold War: Incubators of Contextual Modernism," Avery.

[17] Ibid. See also AIA Gold Medal winners listed in research files. Avery.

[18] Bonnie R. Cohen to The Secretary, *Action Memorandum* on the "Secretary of State's Register of Culturally Significant Property," November 7, 2000. Avery.

[19] Ibid.

[20] Remarks by Secretary of State Madeleine K. Albright at M Reception, Celebrating the establishment of the Secretary of State's Register of Culturally Significant Property, January 4, 2000, distributed by Office of International Information Programs, U.S. Department of State. Avery.

[21] See Wijnand Galema and Fransje Hooimeijer, *Bouwen aan diplomatie, De Amerikaanse ambassade in Den Haag,* Marcel Breuer, 1956–1959. The City of The Hague, Department of Urban Development (Rotterdam) December 2008. In preparation for decommissioning of the Breuer building and the move of the U.S. Embassy to its new campus-like location in the suburb of Wassenaar, the City of The Hague commissioned a preservation study of the Breuer building. That study outlines possible adaptive re-use options for the landmark structure. Much detested locally for many years, it is now beginning to be appreciated as a landmark of mid-century modernism. The City of The Hague will acquire the building as part of the transfer agreement with the USG.

[22] *Effective Diplomacy and the Future of U.S. Embassies:* Hearings of the National Security and Foreign Affairs Subcommittee of the House Oversight and Government Reform Committee, 110th Congress, 2nd Session (January 23, 2008) (statements of Thomas Pickering, former U.S. ambassador and under secretary of State for Political Affairs; Marc Grossman, former U.S. ambassador and under secretary of State for Political Affairs; and Jane Loeffler, visiting associate professor, University of Maryland).

[23] Williams's tenure at OBO was from March 12, 2001 to December 31, 2007.

[24] According to the U.S. Embassy, Manila, the Manila Chancery was established by the Philippine Independence Act passed by U.S. Congress on March 24, 1934, and the Philippine government donated some seventeen acres of land, most of it underwater, for the seaside compound. The *Register* listing suggests that the chancery was built by the USG. That appears to be so, but as the Embassy notes, the project was funded under a special congressional appropriation, probably not under the aegis of the Foreign Service Buildings Commission. Some copies of FSBC records are available in Loeffler Collection, Avery. Six original volumes of FSBC minutes were stored at FBO when viewed there by this author in 1992.

[25] Charles E. Williams to The Secretary, *Action Memorandum* on the "Register of Culturally Significant Property," April 5, 2004. Avery.

[26] Cohen, *Action Memorandum,* November 7, 2000.

[27] Department of State, Bureau of Overseas Buildings Operations, Cultural Heritage Program Symposium: *Saving the Department's Treasures* (October 6, 2008), 31 pgs. Avery.

[28] Ibid.

[29] Ibid.

30 The American Cemetery in Tripoli is a memorial to the thirteen U.S. Navy sailors killed in the explosion of the ketch *Intrepid* off the coast of Libya in the First Barbary War (1804). The property has long been contested ground. The 2004 Normalization Agreement between the United States and Libya established the cemetery as USG property for the first time with the Libyan government agreeing to provide legal protection to the site. The U.S. Embassy oversees it as a diplomatic property under the jurisdiction of the State Department. Veterans groups have protested the arrangement. It is not clear exactly why this property was added to the Secretary's Register, but there must have been a political purpose as its cultural history is still disputed.

31 Columbia University, "Avery Architectural & Fine Arts Library Acquires Jane C. Loeffler Embassy Archives," Press Release (September 3, 2014); and Adil Mughal, "New Avery acquisition brings together diplomatic history, architecture," *Columbia Daily Spectator,* September 22, 2014.

32 Patrick Kennedy, letter in *Saving the Department's Treasures.*

33 Thomas P. Marotta e-mail follow up to Loeffler regarding Tracey interview with Loeffler (November 3, 2015) at OBO, November 19, 2015.

34 City of Westminster, *Listing of Buildings of Special Architectural or Historic Interest,* LS/PP/JH/85860 or MRB/USA/1/2 Schedule listing for United States of America Embassy, Grosvenor Square, 503983 II DCMS (October 20, 2009), Avery.

35 Chris Bourke, "U.S. Embassy Building in London Sold to Qatari Diar," (November 3, 2009), http://www.bloomberg.com; "Revealed: London's £3 BILLION embassy sell-off bonanza," (August 22, 2013), http://www.standard.co.uk; Keith Allen, "Yours for £18m: Flat with a View of Grosvenor Square," (March 13, 2014), http://www.standard.co.uk.

36 See City of Westminster, *Listing.* Three sources are cited in the listing: one short published journal article (1960), one unpublished report from *English Heritage,* (2007), and one book, Loeffler, *The Architecture of Diplomacy* (1998).

37 Arif Belgaumi, "Remembering Neutra's Embassy," *The Express Tribune* (February 21, 2011). See also "The Neutra Embassy Building in Karachi, Pakistan: A Petition to Save Modernism," http://www.archdaily.com.

1. Shirakawago, Japan. Copyright Natsuko Akagawa.

Natsuko Akagawa

Japan and the Rise of Heritage in Cultural Diplomacy
Where Are We Heading?

Matters of heritage have increasingly become an important element in international affairs. While expertise in heritage, in consequence, has become a marketable commodity, the ability of heritage to perform a role in international relations remains contingent on the development of a universally shared understanding on what, in fact, heritage consists of or means and what constitutes "best practice" in performing heritage. Coming to this understanding has been a long historical process, and central to it has been the need to determine universally applicable criteria. This is balanced with a respect for local criteria of authenticity. In this process, as this article will show, Japan has played a crucial role. Japan has also been at the forefront of nations strategically employing heritage in cultural diplomacy. In both cases, its prominent role is indicative of Japan's own historical legislative attention to the conservation of its heritage and the national significance ascribed to that heritage in both the internal and external projection of Japanese identity.[1] Nevertheless, with recent legislative changes allowing Japan's ability to engage in military actions and increased global instability impacting places of historic significance, we cannot but stop to consider where we are heading. Will the future see diminishing funds for culture and increased funds to combat "the enemy," as Japan falls in line with the direction of the West? Or is this in fact precisely the time when cultural diplomacy becomes of greater significance in contributing to global stability and harmonious development, as Japanese academics and the general public have continued to believe in and have worked towards over a number of decades?

In this article I argue that in the second half of the twentieth century Japan has employed its national legislative system on heritage conservation as part of its cultural diplomacy to engage more actively with the international community. Initially this was motivated by a need to reestablish its presence on the world stage after its defeat in World War II. Increasingly, however, Japan sought to harness its own experience and expertise in heritage as a vehicle for the exercise of its influence abroad alongside its rise to economic power. At the same time, "heritage in cultural diplomacy" was presented as an expression of its constitutional principles of seeking peaceful coexistence and harmonious development. Assessment of the significance of heritage in Japanese diplomacy also

Future Anterior
Volume XIII, Number 1
Summer 2016

necessitates consideration of how Japan is perceived as a "heritage nation" by the recipients of its cultural diplomacy as well as the alignment of Japanese heritage practitioners and institutions participating in Japanese-funded heritage projects abroad to their nation's international cultural policy.

The performance of heritage entails a range of technical and administrative skills and aesthetic understandings owned by individuals. It follows that any significance that may be accorded to the performance of heritage in cultural diplomacy is necessarily underpinned by the attribution or at least perception of such expertise. The exercise of cultural diplomacy incorporating heritage in a nation's international relations, therefore, remains dependent on the recognition that such a nation's expertise in the field entitles it to "own" the skills and knowledge that are internationally prized and desired. Even so, the interests of expert practitioners on the basis of whose work the success of cultural diplomacy ultimately depends may not coincide with the political motives of their governmental sponsors. What motivates such heritage experts is unlikely to be lofty nationalist objectives but rather a commitment to academic and professional skills; that a government program facilitates their ability to work abroad may be a happy opportunity.[2] As Ang and Mar have also recently stressed, a consideration of heritage diplomacy must take cognizance of the important gap, both in theoretical discourse and in the "real world," that can exist between the "fundamentally nationalist underpinnings of cultural diplomacy" and the "dialogues and collaboration based on shared interests that are not articulated in the name of the nation-state." Rather than being "actually motivated by such lofty [nationalist] interests," heritage practitioners working on nationally funded international projects are more likely to be motivated by "more concrete purposes such as mutual learning; pooling of resources, co-financing; technical assistance; joint reflection, debate research and experimentation."[3]

An examination of the role of heritage in the broader context of Japan's postwar diplomatic history provides a unique insight into the development of heritage as a major element in international diplomacy.

Japan's Cultural Diplomacy in the Postwar World

In 1951 following the end of World War II, Japan reengaged the international community with the ratification of the San Francisco Peace Treaty and its membership in UNESCO. Five years later Japan was accepted as member of the United Nations. After joining the world body, Japan's diplomacy was declared to be governed by "Three Principles": (1) recognizing the central importance of the United Nations; (2) cooperating with the free world and (3) strengthening Japan's position as a

member of Asia.[4] While its active involvement in world events
was precluded by the Defense Forces Law of 1954, requiring
Japan to maintain good relations with the United States to
guarantee its security, Japan's "contribution to the free world
[. . .] through its economic might and its moderating influence
on the countries of Asia and Africa was welcomed."[5] Membership in UNESCO conformed to these aims and Japan's declared
postwar objective of rebuilding itself as a peace-loving and
democratic state and projecting itself abroad as a cultural
nation.

A focus on Asia characterizes the early years of Japanese
involvement in heritage conservation–related projects through
bilateral cultural aid programs. This involvement grew from
Japan's prior engagement with the countries they had occupied
in the course of the Pacific War in negotiations over reparations
mandated under the terms of the San Francisco Peace Treaty of
1951. Among the first of these agreements was the settlement
with Burma in 1954, the Philippines in 1956, Indonesia in 1958,
and Vietnam, Cambodia, and Laos (through 1959). Negotiations over war reparations proved more difficult with Thailand,
Malaysia, and Singapore, and were not completed until the
1960s. These agreements typically concerned aid packages
involving the delivery of Japan-made products. As Sakamoto
Kazuya points out,

> All of Japan's reparations were in the form of the provision
> of products and services. The Japanese government placed
> orders with Japanese companies for goods and services
> amounting to the total cost of the reparations and pro-
> vided them to the receiving countries. Japan's reparations
> to the countries of Southeast Asia were thus an effective
> way to promote Japan's economic recovery in that they led
> to domestic production and exports through government
> support.[6]

At the same time, Japan was gradually beginning to take an
active role in international heritage projects through its membership in UNESCO, although initially this was limited largely
to providing financial support, such in its early involvement in
the "Save the Monuments of Nubia" campaign in the 1960s.
However following Japan's involvement in the international
campaign to safeguard the temple of Borobudur, inaugurated
in 1974, Japan became more actively involved internationally in
heritage restoration projects.

Japan's growing diplomatic role, both regionally and
globally, as "Asia's only developed country" coincided with,
and was patently contingent on, its emerging international
position as "a major economic power supporting the world

economy."[7] Representing a ready extension of existing aid programs negotiated as part of its reparation obligations, Japan's financial and increasingly technical support for heritage-related projects formed an important element in this development. The first large-scale heritage projects were in Southeast Asia, initiated in Burma (1975–77 after which further involvement was suspended) and Thailand (1978 onward). Cooperative projects with the South Asian nations followed, with India and Bangladesh (1978 onward), Sri Lanka (1980), and Pakistan (1983). These projects clearly express and helped to promote the image of Japan abroad (once again) as a leading power in Asia. While directly serving its own economic interests, the deployment of heritage as a key element in Japan's cultural diplomacy also involved more than the development of stronger relations and trade with its immediate neighbors; it was also a strategic response to the internal political conditions of the countries concerned while simultaneously meeting broader international expectations in the context of the Cold War. Support for national heritage projects, in particular where it involved iconic manifestations of national identity that had preexisting international recognition, came to represent important contributions to the consolidation of political stability and economic reconstruction in the nations involved.

This is apparent in the case of countries ravaged by the long, drawn-out U.S.–Indochina War, where Japanese support for heritage projects formed part of a broader initiative to restore regional security. While constitutionally prohibited from participating in military activity, following the adoption of the United Nations Peacekeeping Cooperation agreement by the Japanese Parliament, Japan became involved in providing medical assistance, refugee repatriation support, infrastructural assistance, and election monitoring in various international trouble spots, including a major role in UN Peacekeeping operations in Cambodia. In Cambodia, subsequent to the UN-negotiated political settlement there, Japan embarked on a major long-term heritage project for restoration for the Khmer heritage site of Angkor, arguably providing a major boon to that country's economic rehabilitation.

As in the case of Cambodia, Japan also contributed to extensive and continuing involvement in the development of Vietnam's heritage policy and practice until 1989. The focus of this case was the historic precinct of Hoi An and Hue, which followed Vietnam's political stabilization after the unification. The signing of a heritage cooperation agreement with China in 1982 for the development of the Dunhuang heritage site represented an important element in Japan's contribution to the reestablishment of diplomatic links of a post-Maoist China with the international community.

2. Hue, Vietnam. Copyright Natsuko Akagawa.

In each of these cases, long-term self-interest on Japan's part is also clearly evident. In the case of China, for instance, while engaging with Japan suited the internal political PRC agenda as it shifted its cultural focus from its now-discredited Maoist past, for Japan a more open China represented an important economic opportunity. In the case of Korea, where officially sanctioned expressions of resentment for its wartime

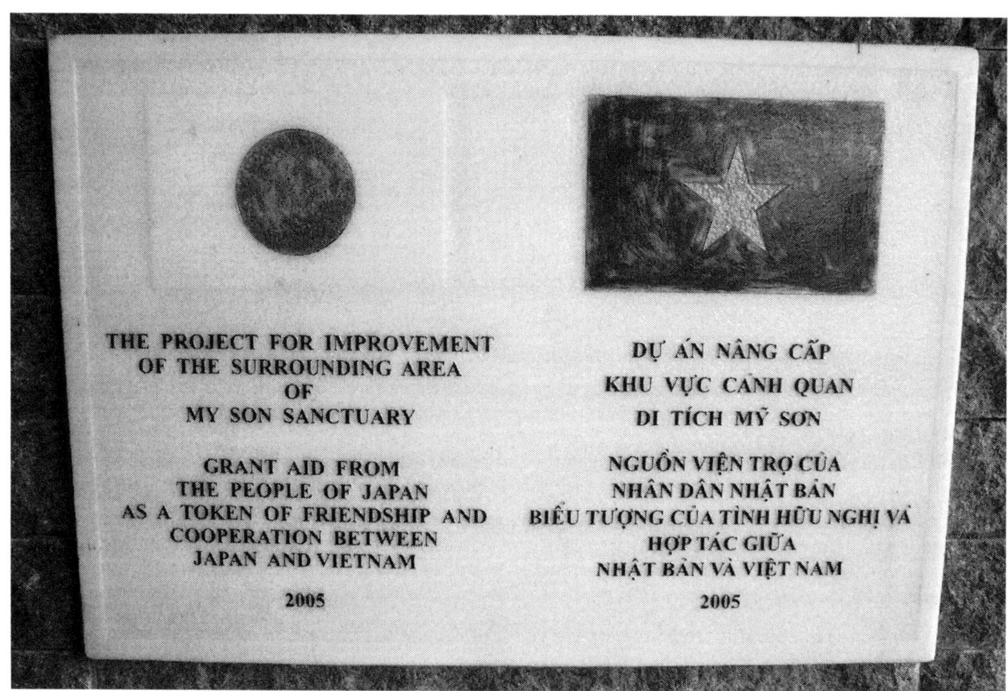

3. My Son, Vietnam. Copyright Natsuko Akagawa.

experience under Japanese occupation had been ongoing, heritage cooperation followed close on the heels of the normalization of relations in late 1989. The first agreement was signed in 1990, significantly coinciding with the lifting of the Korean ban on Japanese imports. A decade later, Japan also signed an agreement with North Korea for an extensive eight-year joint research project on the third century BC Koguryo historic sites.

Beyond these more pragmatic political and economic considerations, the latter projects in Northeast Asia—as well as those in South Asia—are also evidence that Japan's heritage diplomacy directly involved the national cultural interests of Japan itself. From the early 1970s, Japanese experts had begun to carry out archaeological surveys in Afghanistan, China, Kyrgyzstan, India, Nepal, Pakistan, Tajikistan, Uzbekistan, and Turkmenistan. Many of these projects were built on earlier, prewar Japanese research into the origins of Japanese civilization and peoples, believed to have originated in south and central Asia and migrated to Japan through Mongolia, China, and the Korean peninsula millennia earlier. Prewar archaeological research in Korea and the development of a heritage legislative system in the colonial era (which form the basis of current heritage-related legislative mechanisms in Korea) had all been directed to this end.[8] Interest in Afghanistan, where Japanese activity commenced in 1976, centered on the important sixth-century Buddhist site at Bamiyan and the extensive Kushan Empire of the third century AD that was in power in the region covering present-day Afghanistan, another focus of prewar Japanese research. This had to be terminated with the Russian invasion in 1979. Elsewhere in Southeast Asia, notably in Indonesia and Vietnam, Japanese archaeologists had also shown an interest in early Buddhist and Hindu architectural antiquities before and during their wartime occupation. In Indonesia during the period of Japanese occupation, Japanese experts continued archaeological research initiated by the Dutch and intervened directly to safeguard sites of architectural significance from damage by Japanese military activities.[9]

Cultural Diplomacy since the 1980s

While a sharp distinction cannot be drawn, it is apparent that the 1980s marked a significant acceleration in Japan's cultural diplomacy. It saw a notable extension of interest beyond Asia, but more particularly, the beginning of a more concerted policy of cultural assistance, consisting of both financial and technical aid, in support of heritage conservation. Although again heritage-related activity largely took the form of providing manpower and facilities, attention was now focused increasingly on what at the time was referred to as "the Third World," in particular Africa, which in the 1980s was considered to be a continent in crisis.[10]

Coinciding with its position as the world's second-largest economy, Japan embarked on what Prime Minister Takeshita Noboru declared to be Japan's international cooperation initiative. This initiative supported cultural projects as its central element. The initiative was intended to reflect Japan "recognizing deeply its increased international responsibility and role" as a "member of the Western community of nations and of the Asia-Pacific region" and aimed to "create a 'Japan Contributing to a Better World.'"[11] This rather grand statement was backed by a commitment to an Overseas Development Aid program to support world cultural heritage projects and provide active support for international cultural exchanges. The National Research Institute for Cultural Properties oversaw the heritage expertise the country was to disseminate abroad. Founded in Tokyo in 1930 as a center for the development of technical expertise, the Institute continues to conduct seminars, support the training of overseas heritage practitioners and to undertake research. State driven cultural diplomacy was thus aimed to directly connect the country's institutional and professional heritage experts with the implementation of its cultural diplomacy policies.

This shift in Japan's diplomatic profile was in large part a response to international pressure from the West. Caught in the crosshairs of Cold War rhetoric, Japan had increasingly become a target of US-led "Japan bashing". Cold war politicians in the US had long accused Japan of obstructing US policy not only in the "fight against communism" and its anti-Soviet strategies,

4. Hiroshima, Japan. Copyright Natsuko Akagawa.

but also in its pursuit of economic policies. Japan was accused of "tak[ing] a free ride on the United States for its own military security" on the basis of Article 9 of its constitution, while at the same time failing to open its economy to "free trade" in support of its allies' economic and political interests.[12] In the Cold War rhetoric of the day, for the United States "one either becomes an ally or becomes an enemy."[13]

In the face of such international pressure, right-wing elements inside Japan agitated for a review of the country's pacifist constitution. This, however, was resisted, and reflecting the overwhelming support of the Japanese public, the Japanese government instead reiterated its earlier "Three Principles" that underpinned Japan's commitment to peaceful diplomacy. This diplomacy focused on economic and cultural cooperation in which support for heritage came to play an increasingly important role and could be shown to be aligned with a concern for "Third World" development, the major narrative in political science discourse in the West at the time, as well as reflecting Japanese national ideals.[14]

Japan and the Internationalization of Heritage Practice

While Japan developed strategic policies to build relations with "developing economies," the country fulfilled both international (Western) expectations and the principles of its constitution. Japan also pursued the development of its international profile through UNESCO. Japan's voice in international heritage discourse had become increasingly prominent since hosting UNESCO's Nara Conference in 1992. Following the UNESCO Recommendation on the Safeguarding of Traditional Culture and Folklore of 1989, the Nara Conference had been arranged to focus the attention of world experts on the question of the universal application of the principle of "authenticity" in heritage conservation. Its outcome, the Nara Document on Authenticity (1994), signified a seismic shift in modern heritage theory and practice toward a more diverse and complex understanding of heritage and its safeguarding by balancing the principles of "authenticity" and "universality."[15] This had become more than an academic issue at the time—it impinged directly on a larger political question, arguably promoted by the end of the Cold War and the last vestiges of European imperialism. It concerned the continuing Eurocentrism in notions of "universal value," and specifically the Eurocentric bias in existing conceptions of world heritage embedded in the 1972 Convention Concerning the Protection of the World Cultural and Natural Heritage (World Heritage Convention). Assumptions underlying this governing device, it came to be recognized, "needed to be re-examined [in order that] heritage conservation can be seen to have global significance and be guided by truly global precepts."[16]

Japan played a major role in the recalibration of international discourse on heritage toward developing a more universal basis for the identification and approach to the conservation of heritage of world significance. As well as claiming the success of its own tradition in national heritage legislation and conservation policy, it also argued that its approach to heritage reflected principles that were more in common with those of its Asian neighbors. Subsequently, in the development of the UNESCO Convention for the Safeguarding of the Intangible Cultural Heritage, adopted in 2003 under Japanese Director General Matsuura Koichi and coordinated with support from the Japanese government, the criteria for identifying world heritage of significance was officially declared to include "intangible" heritage. This, it was agreed, recognized widespread practice of those non-Western countries, including Japan, "whose heritage is expressed more typically through cultural expression, namely music, dance, and oral traditions."[17]

While the attempt to accommodate different cultural forms and nonforms within a concept of heritage has resulted in greatly complicating the practice of safeguarding heritage, it has also ensured that the identification and conservation of more vulnerable elements of heritage has increasingly become a matter of specialist expertise and strategic national and international guidelines, and, in consequence, increasingly a significant element of the knowledge economy. Japan's leadership in recasting the international heritage discourse, and its perceived expertise based on a long history of heritage conservation practice upon which this was based, was able to influence international practice and thus strengthen the efficacy of

5. Hue, Vietnam. Copyright Natsuko Akagawa.

employing heritage in its cultural diplomacy. At the same time, the broadening of accepted principles of defining heritage ensured that aid recipient countries were more receptive to Japanese diplomatic approaches regarding heritage projects.

Since the 1990s, having established its leadership role in international heritage practice, Japan has focused on initiating major long-term heritage-related projects in a wide range of countries. These have been explicitly developed within the broad framework of "Interregional Cooperation" involving "human resource development." Warmly welcomed by the countries concerned, which were themselves well advanced in deploying heritage as symbols of national identity in strategies for achieving national unity and development, such projects also contributed to Japan's broader economic interests in developing relations with major suppliers of raw materials and markets for its exports. In this sense, "heritage diplomacy" clearly formed part of the exercise of Japan's "soft power," understood in the concise sense as the deployment of values central to its culture in the pursuit of an overall foreign-policy framework perceived to reflect those political values.[18]

Indonesia and Vietnam provide prominent examples of such long-term, detailed, cooperative projects that concurrently met the mutual economic significance of both parties. Indonesia, for instance, where Japan has been involved in two major heritage projects, currently represents a major destination for Japanese exports while, for Indonesia, Japan is its third-largest source of imports.[19] Heritage projects here have included an extensive three-year planning survey of its major Hindu temple site of Prambanan (2006–8) and a longer-term conservation project of the former royal palace of Sumbawa, both monuments of iconic national significance. Of particular interest in the latter project, a "Cooperative project for the Conservation of Traditional Wooden Buildings" in the context of "Cooperation for the Conservation and Restoration of Cultural Properties and Buildings in the Asia-Pacific Region," is its reliance on a unique aspect of Japanese heritage expertise: conservation and restoration of wooden buildings. In Vietnam, Japan has been involved the conservation of its Hoi An heritage site since the early 1990s in a series of nine separate projects of varying lengths. Project aims range from providing "fundamental research," to undertaking planning surveys, to conservation and restoration work involving human-resource training, to developing "awareness raising and promotional" programs. For Vietnam, Japan also represents a major destination for its exports, second only after United States, and the third-largest source of its imports.[20] Over a similar time span, Japan has also developed a series of cooperative projects with Cambodia focused on the significant Khmer site of Angkor.

As Japan's own economy expanded in the course of the twentieth century, its development aid increased in terms of range, amount, and geographical spread. By the end of the century Japan had become the world's largest bilateral aid donor.[21] At the beginning of the twenty-first century, Japan reiterated its aim to have international cultural aid as its key principle underpinning its activities in the international arena. As expressed in the Official Development Assistance (ODA) Charter of 2002,

> Japan will give priority to assisting developing countries that make active efforts to pursue peace, democratization, and the protection of human rights, as well as structural reform in the economic and social spheres.[22]

"Heritage aid" has demonstrably played a central role in the realization of this policy. Between 1978 and 2015 the Japan Centre for Intercultural Communications (established 1953), designated as the instrument for the conduct of international heritage projects, has coordinated a total of 799 heritage-related projects. While statistics demonstrate the emphasis of its focus on Asia (488 projects), it also reveals significant engagement in the Middle East (116), South America (80), Europe (64), and Africa (51).[23] Expressive of its own history, the prominence given to its role in the international articulation of the protocols of heritage governance, and participation in international heritage projects reflects Japan's own approach to heritage in focusing national sentiment. And, indeed, while the heritage-conservation projects have contributed directly to economic development, primarily by providing new sources of income from tourism, and contributing to political stability by underscoring of the national significance of iconic heritage sites in "developing countries," heritage diplomacy has also helped focus national sentiment at home. More than a rhetorical flourish lay behind Prime Minister Aso's characterization of Japan's diplomatic policy as an example of Japan

> working hard on the ground together with the local people while spreading the very concept of joy in labor. It is about aspiring to create a cultural base which will facilitate the independence of the aid recipient country through these acts.[24]

International policy is, in other words, seen (or at least rhetorically presented as) an extension abroad of Japanese national character and ideals.

Conclusion

Attention has increasingly been directed to the "credibility gap" that can emerge in the pursuit of a nation's cultural diplomacy between the projected image and the reality. Another such "gap" can be found between the pursuit of national cultural diplomacy and that which is involved in the activities of individuals operating independent of, or outside the ambit of, national policy that has been defined as the deployment of "public diplomacy."[25] What becomes evident in a survey of the exercise of Japan's cultural diplomacy, particularly as it applies to activities in the field of heritage, is the symmetry between the pursuit of cultural diplomacy and the ideals of the Japanese nation. It is equally evident that the pursuit of cultural diplomacy is unashamedly an integral element of the broader economic and political goals of the nation. In the case of Japan, the exercise of "soft power," as Nye envisaged the concept, can therefore be seen as being a crucial element in Japan's international relations, and within this heritage plays a central role. Finally, although space has precluded examination in detail of Japanese-assisted heritage projects, it is also evident that, "on the ground," the work of Japanese heritage experts has been crucial to, and has consistently been in alignment with, these national goals.

It remains to be seen whether existing trends in heritage practice will or can continue. Scenes of the destruction of millennia-old buildings, increasingly rapid deterioration of natural landscapes under pressure of climate change, economic development, population shifts, and deliberate destruction — not to mention the brutal acts targeting the custodians of culture and heritage, the academics and curators involved — raise fears of whether this form of diplomacy that involves the

6. Hiroshima, Japan. Copyright Natsuko Akagawa.

cooperative work of UNESCO's member states will be able to maintain the achievements of the past. Japanese heritage–related activities in the war-affected countries Iraq, Syria, and Afghanistan, which since 2000 have represented Japanese contributions to postconflict stabilization in lieu of direct military assistance, have all been interrupted by recent escalations of conflict in these countries. The recent decision to modify the prescriptions of Article 9 of its constitution mandating Japan's nonmilitary stance in international affairs—despite overwhelming popular support from a Japanese public for its maintenance—may lead to a possible redirection in its international diplomacy, as resources of a declining economy are redirected toward other political objectives. Also of concern in the light of the most recent events are signs that disagreement with policies adopted by the world body can influence member states to withhold funding to UNESCO. Japan has recently indicated the possibility that it would withhold funding after disputing a UNESCO decision to adopt a Chinese proposal to have documents related to the Nanjing massacre nominated to the Memory of the World register established in 1992.[26] Precedent for such action occurred in mid-1980s with the departure of the United States, the United Kingdom, and Singapore following disagreement on UN policy. Although all eventually rejoined, more recently the U.S. funding of UNESCO was again suspended in 2011 following a similar "unacceptable" decision by the UN, which "has plunged it into a funding crisis and forced it to cut programs."[27] It was Japan's willingness to step into the breach following the earlier departure of the United States and the United Kingdom that enabled UNESCO to continue to develop its activities. Today, given the prominent role it has filled in UNESCO in terms of policy direction and projects as well as financially, even a partial withdrawal by Japan raises the question of UNESCO's vulnerability to global conflict at the diplomatic level, as well as on the ground, and the significance of heritage in the cultural diplomacy of member states.

Finally, a survey of the history of Japan's cultural diplomacy suggests that whether cultural aid is deemed effective will depend on the political interests of both donors and recipients at the time. How one measures "success" or "usefulness" of such diplomacy given this political dimension remains problematic. But what can be said is that the actors and projects, the frontline academics and heritage practitioners, involved in such projects abroad with genuine goodwill, themselves are able to exercise "soft power." As numerous interviews with counterparts in recipient countries continually attest, the educational and emotional engagement generated by cooperative heritage ventures, where these involve investment in iconic emblems of the host nation's identity, can generate a powerful energy to bond people from diverse backgrounds and places.

Biography

Dr. Natsuko Akagawa is tenured at The University of Queensland, Australia. Her recent monograph *Heritage Conservation in Japan's Cultural Diplomacy* (2014) establishes the theoretical nexus between the politics of heritage conservation, cultural diplomacy, and national interest. She is coeditor of *Intangible Heritage* (2009) and of an entirely new second edition forthcoming in 2017. She is also author of *Intangible Heritage and Embodiment: Japan's Influence on the Global Heritage discourse* (2015). She has been visiting researcher at the East West Centre, University of Hawai'i, Manoa, International Institute of Asian Studies/Leiden University (Netherlands), and guest lecturer at Goethe-Universität Frankfurt am Main and other universities. She is Expert Voting Member for International Council on Monuments and Sites (ICOMOS) and Vice-President of ICOMOS International Scientific Committee on Intangible Cultural Heritage. She is also listed as Japanese heritage expert by the Government of the Netherlands.

Notes

[1] Natsuko Akagawa, *Heritage Conservation and Japan's Cultural Diplomacy: Heritage, National Identity and National Interest* (London: Routledge, 2014), 189.

[2] Ibid..

[3] I. Ang, Y. R. Isar, and P. Mar, "Cultural Diplomacy: Beyond the National Interest?" *International Journal of Cultural Policy* 21, no. 4 (2015): 365–81 at 369–70.

[4] Kazuya Sakamoto, "Conditions of an Independent State: Japanese Diplomacy in the 1950s," in *The Diplomatic History of Postwar Japan,* translated and annotated by Robert D. Eldridge, ed. Makoto Iokibe (London: Routledge, 2011), 67.

[5] Ibid., 68.

[6] Ibid., 67–68.

[7] Hiroshi Nakanishi, "Overcoming the Crises: Japanese Diplomacy in the 1970s," in *The Diplomatic History of Postwar Japan,* ed. Iokibe, 138.

[8] Hyung Il Pai, *Heritage Management in Korea and Japan: The Politics of Antiquity and Identity* (Seattle: University of Washington, 2013).

[9] Masatoshi Iguchi, *Java Essay: The History and Culture of a Southern Country* (Kidsworth Beauchamp: Matador, 2015).

[10] Colin Legum, William Zartman, Steven Langdon, and Lynn K Mytelka, *Africa in the 1980s: A Continent in Crisis* (New York: McGraw–Hill, 1979).

[11] Makoto Iokibe, "Japanese Diplomacy after the Cold War," in *The Diplomatic History of Postwar Japan,* ed. Makoto Ikibe, 179.

[12] Radha Sinha, *Japan's Options for the 1980s* (London: Croom Helm, 1982), 234.

[13] Ibid., 227.

[14] See, for instance, Legum et al., *Africa in the 1980s,* 1979; Arthur Gavshon, *Crisis in Africa: Battleground of East and West* (London: Penguin, 1981); P. Wiles, ed., *The New Communist Third World: An Essay in Political Economy* (London: Croom Helm, 1981); Diana Conyers, *An Introduction to. Social Planning in the Third World*

(Chichester, UK: John Wiley, 1982); Robert K Olson, *US Foreign Policy and the New International Economic Order: Negotiating Global Problems, 1974–1981* (London: Frances Pinter. 1981); Karl P. Sauvant, *Changing Priorities on the International Agenda: The New International Economic Order* (Oxford: Pergamon, 1981); Timothy M. Shaw and Kenneth A. Heard, eds. *The Politics of Africa: Dependence and Development* (London: Longman, 1979).

[15] Akagawa, *Heritage Conservation and Japan's Cultural Diplomacy.*

[16] Herb Stovel, "Consideration in Framing the Authenticity Question for Conservation," in *Nara Conference on Authenticity in Relation to the World Heritage Convention, Nara, 1–6 November 1994, Proceedings,* ed. Knut Einar Larsen, 393–98 (Paris: UNESCO World Heritage Centre, 1995).

[17] Matsuura Koichiro ,(松浦 晃一郎). "無形文化遺産の保護に関する条約の発効を記念して [To celebrate the entry into force of the Convention on the Protection of Intangible Cultural Heritage]," *ACCU News Letter* [in Japanese], no. 5, 2006.

[18] Ang et al., "Cultural Diplomacy," 367–68.

[19] Alexander Somoes, "Learn More about Vietnam," *The Observatory of Economic Complexity 2015,* http://atlas.media.mit.edu/en/profile.

[20] Ibid.

[21] Carol Lancaster, "Japan's Oda: Naiatsu and Gaiatsu," in *Japanese Aid and the Construction of Global Development: Inescapable Solutions,* ed. David Leheny and Kay Warren, 29–53 (New York: Routledge, 2010).

[22] Akagawa, *Heritage Conservation and Japan's Cultural Diplomacy,* 86.

[23] Information provided by National Research Institute for Cultural Properties in 2014.

[24] Taro Aso, "Speech by Minister for Foreign Affairs Taro Aso ODA: Sympathy Is Not Merely for Others' Sake," Japan National Press Club, January 29, 2006, http://www.mofa.go.jp/announce/fm/aso/speech0601–2.html, [Original Speech in Japanese with Official Translation in English].

[25] See, for instance, the discussion in Ang et al., "Cultural Diplomacy."

[26] Kiyoshi Takenaka, "Japan May Halt Funds for UNESCO over Nanjing Row with China," *Reuters,* October 13, 2015, http://www.reuters.com/article/2015/10/13/us-japan-china-nanjing-idUSKCN0S70G320151013.

[27] Alexandria Sage and Marine Pennetier, "US, Israel Lose Voting Rights at UNESCO over Palestine Row," *Reuters,* November 8, 2013, http://www.reuters.com/article/2013/11/08/us-unesco.idUSBREA9A701320131108.

Book Review
Diane Siebrandt

U.S. Cultural Diplomacy and Archaeology: Soft Power, Hard Heritage

Christina Luke and Morag M. Kersel
Routledge, 2013

Christina Luke and Morag Kersel, both with backgrounds in field archaeology, worked for the U.S. Department of State in the early 2000s. Their book, *U.S. Cultural Diplomacy and Archaeology: Soft Power, Hard Heritage* investigates how U.S. government efforts in cultural diplomacy are practiced through projects that promote the preservation and conservation of archaeological sites and cultural heritage venues in foreign countries. The goal of the book is to "investigate the avenues in which archaeology is used to further US foreign relation and diplomatic goals" (18). Luke and Kersel provide a comprehensive overview and understanding of cultural heritage programs that are supported and funded by the U.S. government's so-called soft power projects, which assist in promoting and maintaining friendly cross-cultural relations. As someone directly involved in several of the projects they list, I was excited to see this book in print. Most of these projects do not receive the amount of recognition they deserve, such as the Iraqi Cultural Heritage Project, which not only assisted with refurbishments at the Iraq Museum (Figure 1), but also created *The Iraqi Institute for the Conservation of Antiquities and Heritage* (Figure 2). It is refreshing to see them highlighted in Luke and Kersel's narrative of how they support cultural diplomacy.

Confronting what for the layperson can often be a confusing tangle of U.S. government program names and concepts, Luke and Kersel separate the initiatives into specific chapters, listing the histories and inceptions of the programs. For example, they discuss and critique the Council of American Overseas Research Centres (CAORC), which are foreign research centers dotted across the globe that support U.S. policy in diplomatic relations via cultural heritage programming. Information about the centers is useful, yet they do not fully discuss the history of Orientalism in many of the countries where these centers are located. For example, while the centers do indeed promote international scholarly exchange, care must be taken in postcolonial countries where a history of nonnative scholars guiding research agendas exists. In Iraq alone, large-scale excavations in the early twentieth century under the auspices of Western archaeologists resulted in mass quantities of artifacts shipped to Western museums without local consent. However, as part of their discussion of issues related to obtaining

Future Anterior
Volume XIII, Number 1
Summer 2016

1. The Iraq Museum. Photograph by Diane C. Siebrandt.

2. The Iraqi Institute for the Conservation of Antiquities and Heritage. Photograph by Diane C. Siebrandt.

excavation permits, Luke and Kersel do highlight the potential hazards of government expropriation, which they state "often perpetuate the colonial underpinnings" of archaeology (57).

Luke and Kersel provide a detailed narrative on pairing different U.S. government departments, such as the U.S. Department of Homeland Security, with foreign countries in

3. Looted site in southern Iraq.
Photograph by Diane C. Siebrandt.

order to curb looting of archaeological sites (Figure 3). They also highlight important projects that assist authorities in the recovery of looted antiquities, such as the U.S. government-funded International Council of Museum's (ICROM) Red List, which details objects that are most likely to be plundered from sites (Figure 4). The authors tend to support such partnering in the name of promoting positive soft-power diplomacy across cultural lines.

Luke and Kersel provide details about how such U.S. policies function. For example, because a Ministry of Culture does not exist within the U.S. government, the Cultural Heritage Center (CHC), housed within the Department of State's Bureau of Education and Cultural Affairs, acts as the de facto cultural entity in the United States. The authors often discuss the image of the U.S. government that is presented to foreign countries and their populations, stating that the work generated by the CHC gives the United States a positive image (81). However, they also critique some programs that proved problematic in the past, such as a 2007 meeting that involved members from numerous countries concerned with cultural heritage issues, and how the topic of looting created a disconnect between what the participants wanted to depict to foreign audiences and the goals of the program, which were site protection, border security, and museum inventories (84). Background knowledge such as this can be helpful to any scholar weighing the options of whether to work with governmental agencies.

The authors do not discuss the rather controversial issues surrounding archaeologists and cultural heritage specialists

who work with the U.S. government, specifically the U.S. military. A wide divide in opinion exists within the cultural heritage community as to whether partnering with military forces is ethically appropriate. Although this hot topic has been noted and argued by many scholars, including Rene Teijgeler (2008), Yannis Hamilakis (2010), John Curtis (2011), Laurie Rush (2011), Peter Stone (2011), and Joris Kila and James Zeidler (2013),[1] the issue is relevant to many of the programs and projects Luke and Kersel discuss. However, they do talk about the Cultural Antiquities Task Force (CATF), which contracted with the University of Pennsylvania Museum of Archaeology and Anthropology to train U.S. Customs agents in the recognition of antiquities. According to Penn scholars, the U.S. governement's control over the program made them uncomfortable, so they ended their involvement with the program, which was later taken on by the Smithsonian and the National Parks Service, also government organizations (96).

The book's narrative overall welcomes the use of government funding for cultural heritage initiatives, but also raises questions of possible uses of money that may bias research. For example, the Ambassadors Fund for Cultural Preservation (AFCP), which according to the authors claims to be nonpolitical yet "is another element of the diplomatic toolkit, one that further embeds the discipline of archaeology within the larger US democracy project and cultural diplomacy" (98). Projects at numerous sites have been funded by the program, which has been criticized by some for supporting restorations of mosques and churches in the Middle East and South Eastern Europe, bringing to mind the issue of separation of church and state. The authors discuss whether some decision-making is politically influenced in order to benefit the U.S. government, rather than the site or the local population, but also state that the goal is to create and maintain dialogue and an "open exchange of ideas" (127). Again, this useful input can help steer scholars in making decisions when seeking partnerships within governmental agencies.

The authors also hit on the lack of cultural heritage awareness training within the ranks of Foreign Service Officers (86). More specifically they discuss how members of the U.S. military were unaware of how cultural heritage issues affected the local Iraqi population at the start of the Second Iraq War, and they provide examples of initiatives that have been put in place since 2003. Programs such as cultural heritage awareness playing cards that were distributed to deploying forces were well received by both coalition personnel and the Iraqi heritage professionals (Figure 5). They also provide useful information about new and ongoing initiatives, such as training programs implemented to assist Reserve Officers Training Corps (ROTC) members understand how to engage with local populations (131). The list of programs in the book would benefit any scholar who wishes to research topics related to the U.S. politics of cultural preservation and conservation.

Overall the authors discuss the U.S. government–funded programs as useful platforms for cross-cultural cooperation that should be supported because a nonpolitical, nonmilitary face of the United States is needed for international cross-cultural relations. Luke and Kersel state that the U.S. government programs tend to be proactive rather than reactive (128) and that they are principally positive initiatives that try to move beyond colonial models of "the West is the best" and engage fully with the local community to allow equal partnerships and the exchange of knowledge (130). They summarize the book by stating that there is "a proven track record of mending fences and building bridges through the use of cultural programming, and more specifically, the long-term successes of US archaeologists and archaeology deployed as unofficial ambassadors of goodwill" (138).

5. Heritage Resource Preservation Playing Cards. Photograph by Diane C. Siebrandt.

The types of discussions contained within the chapters would certainly prove useful to any cultural heritage expert, including preservationists and conservators, attempting to comprehend U.S. government's policy and its ties to heritage issues. The information is presented in a manner that makes it possible to understand the nuances involved with U.S. government–funded projects, and to recognize the politics behind the programs. The information contained in the chapters provides scholars with a platform to further investigate if

such programing is right for their projects, or simply to help
understand U.S. government policies and their ties to cultural
heritage issues. As cultural heritage–related issues continue
to stay in the mainstream, specifically when extremist factions
perpetrate wholesale destruction against heritage sites, having
a clear understanding of U.S. governmental policy can help sort
out sometimes confusing strategies.

Biography
Diane Siebrandt is currently a PhD candidate with *The Alfred Deakin Institute for Citizenship and Globalisation,* at Deakin University in Melbourne, Australia. She is looking at heritage–military relations, focusing on the history of Orientalism toward Iraqi archaeological sites, from early nineteenth-century explorers, to U.S./Coalition military forces during the 2003 Iraq War. Prior to coming to Deakin, Diane worked on cultural heritage programs throughout Iraq on behalf of the U.S. government for eight years. She has presented at numerous international conferences and has received several awards for her work in Iraq.

Note
[1] Rene Teijgeler, "Embedded Archaeology: An Exercise in Self-Reflection," in *The Destruction of Cultural Heritage in Iraq,* ed. Peter Stone and J. Farchakh Bajaly, 173–82 (Woodbridge, UK: Boydell Press, 2008), 173–82; Yannis Hamilakis, "From Ethics to Politics," in Y. Hamilakis and P. Duke, eds., *Archaeology and Capitalism: From Ethics to Politics,* 15–40 (Walnut Creek, Calif.: Left Coast Press, 2010); John Curtis, "Relations between Archaeologists and the Military in the Case of Iraq," in *Cultural Heritage, Ethics, and the Military,* ed. Peter Stone, 193–213 (Suffolk, U.K.: Boydell & Brewer Suffolk, 2011); Laurie Rush, "Military Archaeology in the US: A Complex Ethical Decision," in *Cultural Heritage, Ethics, and the Military,* ed. Stone, 139–51; Peter Stone, "Introduction: The Ethical Challenges for Cultural Heritage Experts Working with the Military," *Cultural Heritage, Ethics, and the Military,* ed. Stone, 1–28; and Joris Kila and James Zeidler, *Cultural Heritage in the Crosshairs: Protecting Cultural Property During Conflict* (The Netherlands: Brill, 2013).

Mo Michelsen Stochholm Krag

Artist Intervention
The Controlled Ruin
Preserving Collective Memories through Building Transformation

At the moment most of the countries in the Western world are experiencing severe demographic changes. The population in the rural areas abandon their home villages and move into the cities. In Denmark this social migration is mainly caused by a decline in employment in food production based on farming and the attached industries. While the major cities in Denmark experience population and economic growth, the villages in surrounding rural areas face abandonment and decay.

Despite good intentions, today's widespread EU and state funds for demolition projects generally emphasize the fast eradication of cultural values under the guise of state-authorized cleanup projects. Therefore, there could hardly be a more urgent reason to enable the public discourse with a more nuanced view on abandoned rural houses, alongside with bunkers and spent industrial plants. Today, these bearers of history are associated with the unflattering term "negative cultural heritage," and, unfortunately, this term serves as justification for demolition.

The increasing quantity of abandoned houses in rural Denmark is my object of interest. *The Controlled Ruin* is one of eleven full-scale building transformations that compose the main body in my architectural research. The aim is to reveal and preserve endangered material and immaterial values, such as aspects of cultural heritage, local narratives, and building density in depopulating rural villages. As an alternative to demolition, I attempt to establish a counterpractice of radical preservation based on a series of transformations of abandoned buildings prototyped at full scale in rural environments. The responses of local people are used as a feedback mechanism and considered as real-life peer reviewing and an important impact indicator and supplement to the physical transformations. *The Controlled Ruin* was first prototyped in March 2014. This strategy involves partially demolishing the building and subsequently allowing the remnants to decay naturally.

Building on partial demolition, *The Controlled Ruin* constituted an attempt to compress and subsequently stretch the inherent matter of time in the natural decay process. Given that the rapid incipient stages of decay that follow in the aftermath of abandonment are often considered unsightly, *The Controlled*

Future Anterior
Volume XIII, Number 1
Summer 2016

Ruin sought to eschew these stages of ruination in order to avoid the incitement for complete demolition. A precisely defined partial demolition transformed the abandoned building into a controlled ruin and exposed the building's private history. The private past becoming the public future provoked an exchange of memories of the building. This also triggered a discussion of the merits of privacy among the local people. Subsequent decay of the ruin proved to influence the feeling of the local community. This resulted in the ruin being taken into their care, added to and used for recreational purposes. Hence, the local residents turned the controlled ruin into a picturesque vision of a romantic ruin.

Conventional building preservations often result in interpreted copies of the buildings themselves as physical conceptions of their original state. Conversely, a controlled ruin is capable of temporarily exposing several material-historic epochs simultaneously. These are revealed through the apparent stratification. The radical transformation reinstates the abandoned building as a new and unfamiliar element in the village setting. As such it acts as a catalyst of an exchange of embedded hidden narratives of the building and the place by provoking a distribution of memories among the local residents. The collection of these memories is like a puzzle, which, once assembled, represents a sophisticated collage of varying relations among people, the building, and the place. The controlled ruin at the church constitutes a prototype of a new rural palimpsest. While occupied by the locals, the ongoing exchange of memories continues. Like a palimpsest it slowly turns into something else as a result of the engagement of the local residents or, more likely, of natural decay. Thus, the transformed building will enable the enclosed material history to be redeemed in interplay with the neighboring community. The building loss is then less sudden and, similar to a mourning process, there is time to reveal or preserve narratives of what is lost.

Biography
Mo Michelsen Stochholm Krag is an architect, educator, and researcher born in Aarhus, Denmark. He is a PhD Fellow in Architecture at the Aarhus School of Architecture, Denmark. He holds a Masters in Architecture. He has seventeen years of experience in the private sector as a building architect. He was cofounder of architectural office Krag de Ridder ApS in 2006. He has researched the transformation of depopulating rural villages and experimental practice research since 2010. He reviews new architecture at the Danish architectural trade journal *Arkitekten*.

1. *The Controlled Ruin*, April 2014. One month after transformation. *The Controlled Ruin* was prototyped as an alternative strategy to complete demolition. Photograph by Mo Michelsen Stochholm Krag.

2. *The Controlled Ruin,* April 2014. A controversial context: *The Controlled Ruin* appeared as a competitor in the landscape to the neighboring church. Photograph by Mo Michelsen Stochholm Krag.

3. *The Controlled Ruin*, March 2015. One year after the transformation. The effects of the first winter have slightly changed the ruins appearance in the landscape. Photograph by Mo Michelsen Stochholm Krag.

4. The blue bathtub, April 2014. The private past of the building was suddenly exposed to the public. This provoked an exchange of memories of the building. It also triggered a discussion of the merits of privacy among the local residents. Photograph by Mo Michelsen Stochholm Krag.

5. The blue bathtub, March 2015. The severe effects of the winter caused a negative change in the local attitude toward *The Controlled Ruin*. Consequently, the local community took the ruin into their care. Photograph by Mo Michelsen Stochholm Krag.

6. *The Controlled Ruin,* July 2015. The picturesque: Local residents have re-inhabited the ruin and turned it into a romantic extension to the neighboring cemetery. Photograph by Mo Michelsen Stochholm Krag.

Submission Guidelines

Future Anterior is a peer-reviewed (refereed) journal that approaches the field of historic preservation from a position of critical inquiry. A comparatively recent field of professional study, preservation often escapes direct academic challenges of its motives, goals, forms of practice, and results. *Future Anterior* seeks contributions that ask these difficult questions from philosophical, theoretical, and critical perspectives.

Articles should be 4,000 words, with up to seven illustrations. It is the responsibility of the author to secure permissions for image use and pay any reproduction fees. An abstract (200 words), a brief author biography (around 100 words), and a list of numbered image captions with credits must accompany the text. Acceptance or rejection of submissions is at the discretion of the editorial staff. Please do not send original materials, as submissions will not be returned.

Formatting requirements for the manuscript: Text must be formatted in accordance with the *Chicago Manual of Style,* 16th Edition. All articles must be submitted in English, and spelling should follow American convention. All submissions must be submitted electronically, on a CD or disk, accompanied by hard copies of text and images. Text should be saved in Microsoft Word or RTF format.

Formatting requirements for illustrations: Images should be sent as TIFF files with a resolution of at least 300 dpi at an 8"-by-9" print size. Each image file should be numbered in accordance with the image captions. Figure placement should be indicated clearly in the text, after the paragraph in which they are referenced. Image captions and credits must be included with submissions.

Checklist of documents required for submission:
    __ Abstract (200 words)
    __ Manuscript (4,000 words)
    __ Illustrations (7)
    __ Captions for illustrations
    __ Illustration copyright information
    __ Author biography (100 words)

Please mail all submissions to:
Future Anterior
Historic Preservation Program
Graduate School of Architecture, Planning, and Preservation (GSAPP)
400 Avery Hall
1172 Amsterdam Avenue
Columbia University
New York, NY 10027

Questions about submissions or published articles can be mailed to the above address or to futureanterior@columbia.edu.

www.arch.columbia.edu/futureanterior

Future Anterior
Volume XIII, Number 1
Summer 2016

Become a *Future Anterior* Sponsor

Future Anterior is funded by grants and distributed in the spirit of making knowledge available to everyone. Donations are critical to helping us accomplish this mission. If you would like to become a sponsor, please fill out this page and mail it, with a check payable to Columbia University, to:

Future Anterior
Graduate School of Architecture, Planning, and Preservation
400 Avery Hall
1172 Amsterdam Avenue
Columbia University
New York, NY 10027

Or contribute by credit card online at:
https://giving.columbia.edu/giveonline/?schoolstyle=110

All sponsors will be recognized in each issue of *Future Anterior* and receive a one-year subscription to the journal.

Please check the appropriate sponsorship level:

Individual Sponsor: ❑ begins at $100/year
Institutional Sponsor: ❑ begins at $500/year
Patron: ❑ begins at $1000/year

Name*: ____

Address: ____

____

City: ____

State: ________________   Zip: ________________

Country: ____

Institution/Office: __________________________________

E-mail: ____
*please provide your name exactly as you would like it to appear in print